UNWIND

UNWIND

A CHRISTIAN'S GUIDE FOR BATTLING STRESS,
WORRY, AND ANXIETY

Dr. Tim Atkinson

Zion Press

Zion Press
1601 Mt. Rushmore Rd, STE 3288
Rapid City, SD 57702

Ordering Information:
Quantity sales. Special discounts are available on quantity purchases by corporations, associations, and others. For details, contact the "Special Sales Department" at the address above.

Unwind/Atkinson —1st ed.

ISBN 978-1-63357-326-0

Library of Congress Control Number: 2020937492

First edition: 10 9 8 7 6 5 4 3 2 1

Praise for *Unwind*

Unwind is a refreshing look at an ancient-yet-new, radical way of Christian life. Reading this book is like sitting with a wise friend who offers that rare integration of sound science, deep spirituality, and practical instruction. In a time of spinning anxiety, Unwind offers a clear, alternative path. Atkinson shows the way out for lives held captive to worry as well as the way in for those who simply want a healthier spiritual life.

—**Amy Oden,** Ph.D.
Author of *Right Here, Right Now: The Practice of Christian Mindfulness*
Visiting Professor of Early Church History and Spirituality
Saint Paul School of Theology @ OCU

Atkinson's *Unwind: A Christian's Guide for Battling Stress, Worry, and Anxiety* offers a six-week course in mindfulness fully integrated with Christian spirituality. Week One helps us appreciate that our breath is life from God, Week Two presents the body as the God created an opportunity to sense this present moment, Week Three and Four show, respectively, that love and forgiveness start as an intention, the intention becomes a practice which makes us more caring for others and heals our own wounds, Week Five instills the recognition that gratitude is what unhooks us from negative or anxious thinking, and Week Six shows us that both mindfulness and the Christian life is not about being perfect but about becoming whole, that is, allowing God's grace to enter into our breath, our flesh, our heart, and our mind. Atkinson's book gives clear guidance to mindfulness and directs us to similar audio guidance on his website. There are also many pearls of wisdom for Christian living. After reading one feels greatly encouraged to put that wisdom into practice. I recommend it to all who are interested in the connection between mindfulness and Christianity.

—**Stefan Reynolds**, Ph.D.
Author of *Living with the Mind of Christ: Mindfulness in Christian Spirituality*
Benedictine Oblate of the World Community for Christian Meditation

In a 5G hand-held immediacy of modern life, Dr. Atkinson encourages us to "Unwind." He teaches us how to slow down and rediscover a "head to heart" relationship with Christ. It is grounded in the rich history of Christian contemplative practice and mindfulness-awareness. Read it to change your life.

—**Paul Bane** MDiv
Mindful Christianity Today

Dr. Atkinson gracefully reminds us how an ancient spiritual formative practice can address the modern problems of anxiety and stress. *Unwind* is a refreshing and practical guide for people to explore and reflect on the benefits of the Christian discipline of meditation. Atkinson carefully walks the reader through a biblical perspective and scientific literature to reveal the benefits of daily meditation. Anyone on an intentional journey of discipleship or dealing with stress and anxiety would benefit greatly from the simple practical guides and spiritual formative exercises offered in Unwind.

—**Timothy Bullington**, Ph.D.
Chair of the Ministerial Studies Board
North Arkansas District Church of the Nazarene

For good reason, Richard Foster begins his spiritual classic, Celebration of Discipline, with the discipline of meditation, foundational to spiritual well-being. The Prophets of Scripture were able to hear the voice of God because they found the inner quietude necessary for hearing, the key to spiritual learning, and growth. Dr. Tim Atkinson's *Unwind* fills a void in uniquely Christian meditation literature, providing rich guidance from personal experience that helps lead us all to the quiet place of spiritual and physical wholeness.

—Thomas Nowlin, M-Div.

Unwind is a beautiful gift of self-care and gives thoughtful, research-driven practices towards healthy living that are anchored in the Christian faith. Dr. Atkinson gives a transparent and personal testimony for how mindfulness and meditation can and should be a daily prescription whether for personal therapy or anxiety prevention.

—Chad Tappe, MBA
Vice-President of Central Arkansas Christian Schools
Worship Minister at Central Church in Downtown Little Rock

To my father, the original Dr. A, who wanted to tell the world about the rewards of being a Christian. To my mother, who supported me every step of the way, and then some.

To Tina who reminded me of what love looks like. To David and Elizabeth who still laugh at my jokes. To Chris who helped me through a really tough time.

Contents

Introduction

A Bold Step

About the Book

When we run our lives on automatic, we often miss the subtle moments when stress and worry become intertwined, forming mental and physical holds on our bodies and minds. Living without pause, we set the stage for anxiety to emerge unwittingly until our overall well-being declines. This book is for you if you want to battle stress, worry, and anxiety with mindfulness and meditation, but you are concerned that these practices conflict with your Christian values. In this small volume, allow me to gently guide you through a six-week mindfulness program, sensitive to Christian thought and grounded in Scripture so you can practice without fear or guilt. Here, you learn to *unwind* from the holds of anxiety, worry, and stress on your life. The program is a focused and gradual process where you learn that the conditions you battle are temporary, and you can learn to release them with time. We will move slowly and thoughtfully, and learn to unwind from the mental and physical holds on our lives until we achieve each stage of release and healing.

Over forty million Americans suffer from anxiety, and 37% go untreated due to the lack of access to medical care or the stigma associated with a mental health diagnosis.[1] The evidence supporting the effectiveness of mindfulness for worry, stress, and anxiety is overwhelming, covering forty years of research and thousands of studies that consistently demonstrate meditation and mindfulness work to complement medical treatments for anxiety, or as a stand-alone practice that you can do at home.

This book is unique because I have deep, personal experience with Generalized Anxiety Disorder (GAD), and I can attest that the daily practice of mindfulness finally healed me through a combination of meditation, prayer, and faith. I practiced for several years using traditional, mainstream, and Buddhism-based methods, and I regularly found myself uncomfortable with the words and approaches the teachers used to explain the current wisdom of meditation and mindfulness. Along the way, I modified the training for my Christian mindset, and the results were fantastic. I based this approach on two fundamental principles: (1) "The One who is in you is greater than the one who is in the world" (1 John 4:4), and (2) God created all things for his purposes (Col. 1:16), including meditation.

In the following chapters, I share the six-week Christianity-based program for mindfulness. This book is not about medical advice; you can think of it as a dialog among friends having a living room Bible study with a teacher who has defeated anxiety using a Christianity-based approach to mindfulness and meditation, and I want you to defeat anxiety, too.

Mindfulness the Christian Way

Mindfulness includes the practice of meditation, but the practice of mindfulness itself is the conscious, active awareness of your thoughts, feelings, actions, and behaviors in such a way that you understand with your heart how your actions affect yourself and others. Jesus asks his followers to abide in this way when he says, "Do unto others" (Luke 6:31). You can be mindful informally, while sitting in a meeting, walking down the street, shopping in a store, leading your team at work, or when with your family. From my perspective, the fruits of the Spirit drive the core of Christianity-based mindfulness behavior, and these are love, joy, peace, forbearance, kindness, goodness, faithfulness, gentleness, and self-control (Gal. 5:22-23).

Meditation the Christian Way

Meditation is a deliberate act of focus which, like physical exercise, requires you to show up every day to show improvement. It is the formal, personal act of mindfulness where you set aside a particular time to train your brain to focus on singular objects of awareness. You start with your God-given breath, move to the body, and expand to the other present-moment experiences that God has given us. It is just like exercise for the body, but instead of exercising your muscles to make them stronger, you exercise your mind and soul to reflect the attitudes of Jesus. I believe these behaviors are captured in the command to "be still and know that I am God" (Ps. 46:10). "Be still" means stillness of body, but it also implies stillness of spirit, mind, and soul. Indeed, the Bible gives us insights regarding what we should practice when being still.

Anxiety, Stress, and Worry for This Program

When I worried, I continuously dwelled on negative thoughts. I even worried about things that were never going to happen, which added unneeded extra stress. Anxiety started to emerge. When I worried like this, I would worry automatically, without paying attention to what was going on in my body and mind. When I worried, it seemed like anxiety was just in my mind, but anxiety had also settled into my muscles and body. I carried an unconscious tension in my jaw, shoulders, stomach, and legs. Worry affects the mind, but if it goes unchecked, it can lead to stress. If stress goes unchecked, the body stays in fight or flight mode. I do not believe God intended us to stay in this state of mind because it causes our focus to shift to self and we can lose sight of him. In this program, I refer to stress, worry, and anxiety together because they all work in unison to generate holds on our thoughts and generate tension in the body. In each chapter, we will take a moment to find tension in the body and mind and gently release it.

We can start right now. Just unclench your jaw. Let it hang loose. You do not have to open your mouth to let your jaw hang. Separate the top teeth from the bottom teeth. Raise your shoulders toward your ears, feel the stretch, then slowly drop your shoulders back into place. As you learn to stop and become mindful of the tension in your body and mind like this, you can break the cycle of stress.

Why This Book?

This book is different from other Christian mindfulness books because it focuses on battling anxiety using mindfulness techniques, and not as a general defense of Christian mindfulness. This three-part book covers a complete program for fighting stress, worry, and anxiety. Each week you will ease tension in your body and mind by learning a mindfulness technique, starting with breath and body awareness, then advancing to practices of love, forgiveness, and humility—the more complicated techniques for some of us to learn and practice in daily life.

I hope my perspective as a Christian, professional educator, and certified mindfulness teacher can help you find profound insights into the benefits of regular mindfulness practice. My view blends facts from research with practical Christianity to teach mindfulness and meditation in an accessible way, with no questions and no apologies about using this God-given tool to help you fight anxiety.

The Model in a Nutshell
Part 1
Chapter 1 covers the basics, along with an outline of the book. I placed lessons throughout the text so you can start learning the techniques as you read. In many ways, the text is interactive, and

I invite you to take time to practice when prompted. For instance, in Week 1 of the program, I prompt you to feel the sensations of the breath in your nostrils as you breathe. Try it now. Continue to notice the feelings of the breath as the air moves in and out of your body. With that, you have learned the most basic technique of meditation. Each chapter builds on the next, so by the end of the book, you can create a Christian mindfulness practice that works for you using the tools in the final chapter.

Chapter 2 is the logical pathway to a mindfulness and meditation practice that complements your Christian values without in-depth theological discussion, fear, or guilt. Authors have written entire books defending Christian mindfulness from church history to current practice, but here we use Scripture and cover this defense in a single chapter. I share my testimony about how God gave me meditation and mindfulness to conquer my anxiety; then, I introduce you to the Christian pathways for adopting meditation with a guilt-free approach to healing.

Chapter 3 is a brief presentation of the scientific facts regarding how mindfulness and meditation practices work for the alleviation of stress, anxiety, depression, high blood pressure, and other ailments. I also assert that mindfulness is a suitable complement to your current approaches to alleviating stress and anxiety.

Part 2
Week 1 covers breath awareness as the core meditative practice using simple biblical principles. You will learn to pay attention to the breath as a way to slow down runaway thoughts. You will learn to focus on the breath as the principal weapon against anxiety, discovering the origin of breath, starting when God spoke creation into existence and beyond, so you can pay attention to the breath with your heart and your head.

Week 2 covers body awareness, a more advanced technique that uses simple biblical principles to appreciate the body that

God gave you without judgment or guilt. Feeling where these sensations reside will help you unwind your physical tension. You will learn to use the body's sensations as the objects of meditation, to experience the present moment fully, and to experience what anxiety "feels" like in your body in order to conquer it.

Week 3 covers the advanced practice of love and kindness meditations. These are perfect Christian mindfulness practices and meditations supported by biblical teachings and science. You will learn that showing love and kindness to yourself and others, in a focused, mindful way, helps you become aware of our shared humanity, and to use this awareness to promote your healing. Understanding your shared humanity gives you the tools to unwind from hate and bitterness.

Week 4 covers forgiveness meditations (the most advanced technique, from my perspective). Similar to loving-kindness, this essential act of Christian spirituality is one of the cornerstones of healing in Christianity-based mindfulness practices. In a focused session, you will explore the advanced practice of the mindfulness of forgiving yourself and others, beginning to unwind from resentment on the road to reducing your anxiety.

Week 5 covers gratitude, using studies from the Bible and evidence from science to learn how to deepen your mindfulness practices toward combating anxiety. Gratitude teaches you how to be thankful for what you have, and gratitude is essential for well-being! You will learn to unwind from selfishness.

Week 6 covers humility as a core mindfulness attitude. Here you will learn to meditate on God's commands to be humble and inherit the earth, not for yourself but for others. You will learn to adopt the countenance of Christ and become ever so mindful of his presence in our lives. You will learn to trust him, mindfully, on your way to healing, and learn to unwind from pride.

Part 3

The Epilogue covers how to stay on track, and I provide a six-week planning template and words of encouragement for continued practice. I show you how to build a guilt-free practice with the simple rule of, "It's okay to miss a session!" Don't judge yourself or fret, because when you do, you create more tension! Allow yourself to release judgement gently.

CHAPTER 2

Just Do It – Mindfulness Pathways for the Christian

You can practice meditation and still be a Christian using just four basic principles. In this chapter, I share the pathways I used to capture mindfulness and meditation for the Christian. You can find all you need in the Bible, plain and simple. First, I share my testimony about how I conquered anxiety. Second, I share the "pathways" found in God's message of creation, the Psalms, the Ten Commandments, and the life of Christ that support mindfulness and meditation practices.

My Pathway: How I Learned the Long, Hard Way

In my most profound moments of anxiety and depression, mindfulness and meditation healed me. It is that simple. I believe God sent me a gift, and I used it. Some years ago, after I finished my dissertation, I pushed myself to publish more manuscripts and maintain the faculty's ideal of success, which was basically "publish or perish." I also had two small children and a marriage to attend to, so I started to worry about the little things, the big things, and all the things that had happened or that might still happen. I lost sleep worrying at night, worrying about threats real and unreal. My anxiety held me so tightly that I missed what was going on right in front of my face. Spiraling in worrisome thoughts, I felt trapped, and my health went downhill. Each moment of stress and worry created a hold on me, one right after another, and I unknowingly held onto them and allowed them to keep me trapped. Anxiety settled in and started to affect my work, my home life, and my friendships. I lost some friends along the way, too, because of my self-absorbed worry. I worried so much that I would be distant in my interactions my friends, miss key points in their conversations, and fail to follow up with them when they wanted to get together. Eventually, they stopped calling or emailing. I went through a dark and painful time. The next thing I knew, I was in the doctor's office facing a diagnosis of chronic Generalized Anxiety Disorder (GAD). Over the years, the doctor had me on Prozac, Zoloft, and Effexor, each with their mind-numbing side effects. These medications provided some relief, and I was able to start down the road to recovery, but my goal soon became to get rid of the medicines altogether because I never felt like myself when I took them. They only masked the elements of anxiety, allowing me to ignore them in a haze of chemicals. But I knew the elements were still there, festering, and I did not believe God's plan for me included living a poor quality, painful existence.

One day during treatment, my psychiatrist handed me a book on anxiety, and inside I found different forms of meditation. I was, of course, skeptical of the use of meditation for healing, so I was surprised to see it in such a well-known book based on medical knowledge. As a Christian, I avoided meditation like a lot of other Christians did. However, I was still curious why my psychiatrist would give me a medical book with meditation practices because the world of alternative and complementary treatments was still often avoided in mainstream medicine.

I studied the scientific and medical literature for myself, and I discovered pages and pages of well-designed studies in medical journals showing undeniable proof that meditation and mindfulness work to reduce anxiety and stress. The evidence was overwhelming, covering forty years of research and thousands of studies that consistently demonstrated that meditation and mindfulness change the brain for the better. After that, the scientist in me said to take this evidence to heart, but the Christian side of me was still somewhat reluctant. I had to find a way to get past the confusion. Surely God had created this wonderful gift to use without fear or guilt! I was sure God wanted me free of this pain, so I searched the Bible like I was taking on another research project. There, I found overwhelming evidence that meditation and mindfulness practices are just as Christian as prayer (but a little different!).

I tried the techniques, and after a good two months or so, I realized that meditation was all I needed. Later I dropped the medications under a physician's advice, and I have never felt better. That is my testimony. The Lord healed me through meditation, but that was not the end of the story. When I started meditating and bragging about how much better I felt, my Christian friends admonished me, saying I was being led astray by false idols and philosophies.

"Just trust the Lord," they said. "That's all you need."

I did trust the Lord, and I said silently to myself, "I am not being led astray." From there, I set out on a goal to find a way to practice meditation and not feel as if I were doing something wrong.

I pray that you can also find your way out of stress and anxiety through this absolute gift from God. And if you are still on the fence about mindfulness and meditation as an alternative and complementary option to your current treatments and approaches, just study the following meditation pathways that helped me move beyond doubt and into healing.

Pathway 1: All Things Belong to God

When you start the journey with the belief that God created all things and that he willed the universe into being for his purposes (Col. 1:16; Rev. 4:11), you are setting the stage for Christianity-based mindfulness. God, having created all things, also created mindfulness and meditation his purposes. As a Christian, then, you can claim the right to use meditation within your Christian mindset.

Buddhists have used mindfulness as a means of seeking enlightenment for thousands of years, but that does not mean they own the practice, just like Isaac Newton does not own gravity.[2,3] I do not think my Buddhist friends would argue with me either. At the same time, the Christian mystics and Christian desert fathers also practiced mindfulness and contemplation, so by practicing mindfulness, you are tapping into a deep Christian tradition dating back to the third century AD.[2,3] According to the Bible, God created both gravity and mindfulness, regardless of who on earth discovered them or who started using them first. Gravity works without any human intervention, without a cost or exchange, and this happens irrespective of who named it first. Just settle into the gravity right now. It is free. Feel the force holding you down in your seat. As you do this, you can be confident that God reveals himself to you through creation just like this. It is easy to build our faith, abandon our reluctance, and simply claim mindfulness and meditation (and gravity) as gifts from God.

Pathway 2: The Scriptural Prescription

The Bible contains many references to meditation and mindfulness. Sometimes people interpret these passages to mean prayer. Because the Hebrew term for this action/posture is difficult to render, some translators use the term "meditate," which is interesting because there is also a word for "prayer." I do not think the meaning of "meditate" is lost because the New International Version of the Bible uses the word meditate in several contexts. In Genesis, Isaac was meditating in the field when Rebekah emerged, riding her camel (Gen. 24:63). That might have been prayer. Later, the Lord told Joshua to meditate on the Book of the Law "day and night" (Josh. 1:8), a command later echoed repeatedly in the Psalms. Those references are probably meditation in the mindfulness sense, given that mindfulness is often focused on the fruits of the Spirit. The Psalms further emphasize our understanding of precisely what meditation is in the biblical context. The Psalms teach us (1) how long to meditate, and (2) the subject of meditation.

According to the psalmists, we should meditate daily and all day (but also keep in mind practicality) (Ps. 1:2, 119:97). The subject of meditation should be on God's unfailing love (Ps. 48:9), his mighty and wonderful deeds and works (Ps. 77:12, 119:27, 143:5, 145:5), and his precepts (Ps. 119:15, 119:23, 119:48, 119:99, 119:148). I believe prayer is the regular act of making your requests and thanksgiving to God, and meditation is the regular act of opening your heart through faith to God in a non-striving, faithful stillness. Both are actions that have reactions. God answers prayer through faith, and faith is practiced by sitting still. God works without your intervention, and often your only work is simply to be still, demonstrating your faith that God is doing his work. You must trust God hears your prayers, and it is this focus and trust that leads you to heal. We spend a lot of time asking, hoping, wishing, and striving in prayer, which only adds to our anxiety, but we often struggle to sit still in the presence of God as he does the work that is easy for him. We have a built-in desire to be active and make things happen, but in this case, we do not have to do anything during meditation but focus on the breath, the body, or thanksgiving and love. Non-striving, therefore, is one of the cornerstones of mindfulness and meditation and faith.

Pathway 3: Commandments in Plain Sight!
Considering the psalmists recommended that we meditate on God's precepts, it is revealing to note that the five precepts of Buddhism are practically the same as the biblical precepts. The five precepts are Do Not Kill, Do Not Steal, Do Not Harm, Do Not Lie, and Do Not Intoxicate the Mind. Even though the Ten

Commandments are not clear about "intoxicated minds" directly, other parts of the Bible provide clear evidence that your mind should be clear from both internal and external influences. For instance, "Be alert and of sober mind" (1 Pet. 5:8), and in Proverbs, "Wine is a mocker and beer a brawler; whoever is led astray by them is not wise" (Prov. 20:1). Meditation is the practice of making your mind clear, and regular practice eventually eases the toxic thoughts. All we have to do to practice mindfulness is to follow the Christian precepts and teachings of Jesus as they appear in the Bible. It is not necessary to get bogged down in the idea that you are practicing Buddhism because the act of meditation and the philosophy and religion can be separated and used in a way that works for you. Remember, meditation and mindfulness belong to everyone, so using these tools in a Christian context makes your practice of them Christian.

Pathway 4: Practice What You Preach

Finally, Jesus practiced and preached the attitudes of mindfulness during his time on earth. Our focus, our subject of mindfulness on this earth, should be the other people with whom we share the world. Again, all things were created by God. Mindfulness is a way to focus and open the heart to the longstanding essentials of Christian living such as humility, kindness, forgiveness, non-judgmental thought and action, and non-striving—or surrendering yourself to sit still as God does his work. Jesus consistently lived these attitudes, and we should take them to heart and mind. In other words, we are Christian when we live the teachings of the Bible, and mindfulness practices are the exercises that help us improve our ability to conduct these enduring Christian tasks.

Christians exercising mindfulness will practice the attitudes of seeking out and helping the poor in spirit, those who have suffered loss, those who are meek in might and mind, the hungry, and the people in this world who want to do the right thing (Matt. 5:3-6). At the same time, our approach to mindfulness is to be merciful, pure in heart, and seeking to make peace (Matt. 5:7-9). And what is beautiful about this is that you might find your non-Christian meditators and mindfulness practitioners doing the same things. It is the core of mindfulness practice. Because God brings us all together through the practice of mindfulness for his purposes, we share in good works for people who need our strengths. When we gather together for God's purposes, he abides there with us with grace and comfort, and together we try to make this a better place (Matt. 18:20).

Quick Guide: A Christian Mindset for Meditation:
1. God created ALL things for his purposes.
2. The Psalms tell us how to meditate.
3. The Commandments provide the precepts.
4. Jesus lived and taught the mindfulness attitudes.

CHAPTER 3

Silence Your Inner Critic – The Evidence

In the last five years, over 1,200 scientific articles on anxiety and meditation have appeared in PubMed, the medical research database run by the National Institutes of Health (NIH). Here I want to share with you some of the significant research that supports the effectiveness of mindfulness in combating anxiety. I apologize in advance for those of you who want more than what I have provided here, but I wanted to keep this section brief. We know the evidence supports the effectiveness of mindfulness and meditation in combating anxiety, so I am providing just the highlights.

Just as God gave us doctors to be instruments of healing, he gave us scientists to discover and report on the complexities of his creation. This chapter is an overview of the scientific reports or evidence supporting mindfulness and meditation as proven ways to calm anxiety and other ailments. Despite volumes of publications, science has just scratched the surface of understanding God's beautiful creation. Science uncovers what he already knows, and we are amazed by each discovery. Please take a moment to be in awe of how much we still have left to discover.

I often use the NIH PubMed search engine for medical research because of the focus on health and medicine. Using the search term "mindfulness and anxiety," PubMed reported over 1,800 published studies in just the last ten years. Because you want to learn mindfulness rather than read a book about research, I summarized the results based on rigorous published literature reviews and analyses from PubMed.

I invite you to discover that mindfulness and meditation provide natural, scientifically proven tools to combat anxiety and depression and stress. God built this healing tool into us from the very beginning, and he calls it out in his statement, "Be still and know that I am God" (Ps. 46:10). Because your God-given brain is in your head, mindfulness is there, too. We should use both!

The Whole-Brain

Here are three things about the brain that are important to know: (1) science no longer supports that we only use 10% of our brain, (2) nor does it completely support that the left and right sides of our brain are totally different. More recently, (3) data do not yet fully support the idea that "mirror neurons" contain an innate understanding of another person's actions through simple observation, and that more work needs to be done in this area.[4] The bottom line is, all areas of the brain work together to accomplish tasks, store memories, and to think. When you learn mindfulness, you learn to use your whole brain in service, not just some of it. Faith is a matter of the heart and, indeed, the head.

Early Evidence of Pain Reduction

Mindfulness as a tool for pain and anxiety came on the scene in the US back in 1979 when molecular biologist Jon Kabat-Zinn developed a program called Mindfulness-Based Stress Reduction, or MBSR, a program which became and still is the gold standard for reducing stress and anxiety. In 1982, Kabat-Zinn conducted an MBSR program with patients who reported pain in the back, neck and shoulders, head, face, chest, and the gastrointestinal tract.[5] He found that 65% of the patients who completed MBSR showed a reduction in pain or the perception of pain and also noted decreases in mood disturbances.[5] At this stage, the results were preliminary. Still, in the following years, researchers studied the topic further, and more evidence emerged to support the positive effects of MBSR and other Mindfulness-Based Interventions (MBI) on the reduction of pain, anxiety, depression, and other disorders. Since the publication of these results in 1982, PubMed shows over two thousand studies looking at mindfulness and anxiety at the time of my writing this passage. By the time you read this, there will likely be many more studies.

Reduces Depression, Anxiety, and Pain
Fast forward to 2004. Using meta-analysis techniques, Paul Grossman and colleagues examined twenty of the highest-quality studies in the literature that supported the strength of MBSR in reducing depression, anxiety, and sensory pain,[6] and confirmed that these publications provided consistent evidence that MBSR reduces these conditions. A meta-analysis is a highly rigorous method to determine the quality of the results reported by multiple journals and studies with a high level of statistical confidence. These studies help us summarize the state of the science and are only published in the literature if they follow a rigorous set of standards!

Changes the Brain
Earlier I stated that we use our whole brain in mindfulness. In a study using magnetic resonance imaging (MRI), scientists observed that meditators increased the development of gray matter in the brain where learning, memory, and emotion are activated. In contrast, non-meditators showed no changes in the brain.[7] Because the brain is God's creation, God built this mechanism into us for a reason, and we should harness it.

Improves Psychological Well-Being
In 2011, seven years after the 2004 Grossman meta-analysis above, Keng and colleagues performed a rigorous review of the

literature to examine years of research claiming positive effects of mindfulness on psychological health. They concluded that mindfulness does indeed improve mental well-being.[8] Notably, studies continue to show that mindfulness reduces anxiety and stress using more than one anxiety measurement scale,[9] which confirms that mindfulness meditation reduces anxiety regardless of the number of different ways anxiety is defined in the literature!

Reduces Pain Intensity
Nearly thirty-one years after Kabat-Zinn found a reduction in pain, in 2013, Reiner and colleagues found sixteen rigorous research studies indicating a reduction in pain intensity among meditators in clinical trials,[10] backing up Kabat-Zinn's original 1982 results.

Love and Kindness for Empathy
Concerning meditation that takes into account Christian attitudes of selflessness, sharing, love, and kindness, scientists found evidence that practicing loving-kindness might help us with increased capacity for empathy and compassion.[11] Intuitively, we already know that practicing a behavior helps us improve that behavior. Christians might take loving-kindness for granted, because it is what we do, but it is comforting to have some scientific evidence that supports what we feel in our hearts and minds to be the truth.

Complements Medical Treatment
Some might say, "Why not just try to educate yourself about anxiety?" or "Just relax," or "Go to psychotherapy." We can do all of those things, and we should continue to go to psychotherapy when it is prescribed by a doctor, but we know that mindfulness-based practices perform better than health education, relaxation, and psychotherapy alone.[12] Mindfulness and meditation

support your current approaches to reducing anxiety. I think this includes supplementing your prayers and ministry with mindfulness and meditation. We know if we pray to pass a test, God is more likely to help us pass the test if we study for it. In this case, pray, "Lord, heal me from my anxiety," and follow up with an evidenced-based, God-created method to reduce your anxiety.

Reduces Anxiety in Multiple Conditions

One of the more interesting findings is that mindfulness-based practices also help people with autism, a population that is known to experience hard-to-manage anxiety and depression along with an already stressful life.[13] Scientists have found that paying attention with the mind in this way reduces stress and increases the quality of life in people with asthma,[14] cancer,[15] diabetes,[16] irritable bowel syndrome (reduced symptoms!),[17] and heart failure.[18]

Combats Mood Disorders

Six years after the 2011 Keng study and thirteen years after the 2004 Grossman study, Rodrigues and colleagues reported that the literature continues to show mindfulness as an effective and safe way to combat mood and anxiety disorders based on a rigorous examination of the best studies in the current literature at the time.[19]

Conclusion: It Works

For the sake of brevity, I have only summarized the evidence, because I did not intend for this small manual to cover thousands of studies. If you want to know more, I encourage you to do the research and discover these wonders yourself. I included the results of two literature reviews and one meta-analysis covering twenty years of recent research. The results are indisputable. Mindfulness and meditation work if practiced and maintained as part of a daily health-minded practice. In light of all the evidence, I can attest with extreme confidence that a regular

practice of mindfulness drastically reduced (or perhaps elimi-
nated) my crippling anxiety. I no longer take medications, and I
can cope with stress and anxiety efficiently and healthily. In the
following chapters, I introduce a six-week program. Each week,
I provide more biblical and scientific evidence for each type of
mindfulness practice to support the exercise of being mindful in
a Christian way.

PART 2

The Program

The Breath – Unwind from Continuous Thoughts

You can become a master meditator when you learn that meditation is not about blocking your thoughts, but rather about learning to be aware of your thoughts when they arise in your mind. Paul said, "Those who live according to the flesh have their minds set on what the flesh desires, but those who live in accordance with the Spirit have their minds set on what the Spirit desires" (Rom. 8:5). When your mind runs on automatic, you cease control of it, and you slowly default to your taken-for-granted daily behavior. Your selfish preferences assume control, and this creates a condition of mindlessness, opening you up to creating more anxious holds on your mind and body. You can slow down the automatic processing of daily life; all you have to do is practice finding an anchor of awareness or an object of meditation to which you return each time your mind wanders. Now, a wandering mind is not necessarily a bad thing, but if that is all our minds do, they become very good at wandering. Mindfulness and meditation teach us to learn to sit and observe; teach us to focus on what our attitudes should be; and teach our minds to observe and not participate.

In this chapter, we talk about your breath as your first anchor of awareness and your primary tool for battling stress and anxiety. To enhance this lesson on breath awareness, I invite you to discover what the Bible says about the breath. You will find how the breath and life are connected, and learn how to sit still in each moment, focusing on God's presence through the simple act of observing your breath. There is no need to force the experience of your breath. Each breath will enter and exit your nostrils without any effort on your part, just as God designed it. I provide small tips on breath awareness throughout the lessons, so you can learn this awareness as you read. I encourage you to practice as you go!

Breath Is Life

The breath is an essential anchor of awareness for almost all meditation practices. It connects us to life and the promises of God. The breath also connects us to creation, growth, forgiveness, and spirituality. If you are alive, the breath is always with you. The simple wisdom of breath awareness is important no matter who you are or where you are. I invite you to further focus on the breath and how it connects you to life, God, your neighbors, and your enemies. It is essential to see this connection with enemies as well because we all have enemies, both living and imagined. We have demons on the street, and demons in the mind, and we will conquer all of these demons in the following chapters. Still, in the Sermon on the Mount, Jesus says, "Love your enemies and pray for those who persecute you, that you may be children of your Father in heaven" (Matt. 5:44-45).

The mortality we share binds us together with the rest of humanity, and we might not like the fact that the breath of life also connects us to our enemies. The Bible says we are all subject to the same fate. If it makes you feel uncomfortable to think about your enemies like this, that is okay. When you have feelings like this, that is a good indication that you are alive, and you desire to do the right thing. You are human after all, but God commands us to love our enemies, and the discomfort you feel about this could be negative thoughts, or pride, or resentment, or hate. By unwinding these holds on your mind, you can create a pathway to growth in faith and mental strength. But we do this slowly, deliberately, and with much care. We are here to simply start the process of unwinding from anxiety—a gradual, unhurried process. This involves patience, faith, and practice. Take a moment, now, to experience your breath in your nostrils as you breathe. Breathe in and make note of the sensations involved in the system of breathing. Breathe out; make note of the sensations. It is that simple, and in a sustained session of ten minutes or more, over time, you can experience the benefits of focusing on this object of meditation. But you are also focusing on a gift of creation, built into your mind and body by God, for the purpose of calming the mind.

Inhale: Breath in the Beginning
The breath of life started the human race, for "the Lord God formed a man from the dust of the ground and breathed into his nostrils the breath of life, and the man became a living being" (Gen. 2:7). The nostrils are a focal point in meditation. Take a moment to feel the air moving across your nostrils when you breathe. We experience the breath in our noses and in our throat. We sometimes experience our breath as our stomach rises and falls, or as our chest rises and falls. That breath of life has perpetuated the existence of humanity from the beginning, starting with every cry at birth, and ending with every death, marking the arc of life. Do not be somber about death, as it is a salient representation of the life God gave you, and it is a reminder of your dependence on him. Each breath, in and out, is a gift from God. That alone should help you feel closer to him. As you read, continue to take a moment to feel your breath in your nostrils, or as your chest rises and falls, and become curious about this wonderful machine that God has given you.

The breath of life is part of the cycle of life. When God sent the flood, he said, "I am going to bring floodwaters on the earth to destroy all life under the heavens, every creature that has the breath of life in it. Everything on earth will perish" (Gen. 6:17). Pairs of all the animals that had the breath of life in them came to Noah and entered the ark (Gen. 7:15). The Bible is clear that life is represented by the breath, for animals and humans.

I know this might seem simplistic, but that is the lesson. Quite simply, breath is a reminder of life. And when our busy lives sweep us away, we rarely take the time to notice that our breath is keeping us alive, moment by moment, with no conscious effort on our part. We do not take the time to see that we are a breath away from life and a breath away from death. Each day that we take the time to recognize and appreciate our existence in the "now" with our breath, we can begin to defeat stress and anxiety. During the daily grind, we usually ignore our breath, our thoughts, every single heartbeat, and even people who need our attention. When we turn our focus toward the breath, just at the nostrils, we take the time to be thankful for this expansive gift of life from God. As you learned in Chapter 3, science reveals to us that learning to focus on the breath in extended, focused moments brings profound changes to the mind and reduction in stress and anxiety symptoms. There is a reason God created this tool.

As you are learning, contemplative practices use the nostrils as a focal point for the breath for a reason. 2 Samuel 22:16 talks of the "blast of breath from his nostrils," indicating where the breath of life has power. In Exodus 15:10, the Bible continues to show the power of God's breath of life, saying, "But you blew your breath, and the sea covered them. They sank like lead in the mighty waters." You are connected to this mighty breath because God breathed it first and gifted it to you.

Exhale: Breath in the End
This connection to breath and life is vital for contemplation, reflection, and wisdom, which are critical components of a life of

Christian mindfulness. For instance, after Abraham's long life, the Bible says, "Abraham breathed his last and died" (Gen. 25:8). Ishmael, too, lived to be a hundred and thirty-seven, "breathed his last and died" (Gen. 25:17). In both cases, the last breath resulted in a "gathering of his people." The last breath indicated the time when family and friends were to come together and celebrate the life of their loved one who had just entered the spiritual realm.

Reading on, we learn the last breath is not the final act. It is merely a transition, a handing off of duties, wealth, history, and love to the people that surround you. Rachel breathed her last and was celebrated by her relatives in life (Gen. 35:18). Esau and Jacob were with Isaac when he breathed his last (Gen. 35:29). Later, Jacob breathed his last breath and was "gathered to his people" (Gen. 49:33). The Bible says the breath is there to remind you that each day is precious, and to take notice of this present moment and the people in it. Look around you and see who will celebrate your life when you breathe your daily breath, and when you breathe your last breath. Cherish the moments you have with them each day. Each cycle of breath is a mini celebration of life and a reminder of our connection to others. Life offers you more than your worries, your past, and your future.

Who are the people in your life who will gather around you when you breathe your last breath? Who is with you at this present moment? Send a thought or prayer of thanksgiving and love to them now, or if they are near, reach out and touch them with a loving hand. That is a big part of mindfulness. When you breathe in, you celebrate life, and when you breathe out, you continue the celebration. Can you feel the transition of the in-breath and the out-breath? You might feel your lungs react at each shift. Make a note of those sensations because they are useful for focus. You are not required to make your lungs move. It will happen. When I say "breath," what anchors your mind? Keep these questions in mind as we move forward.

Breath Is Spirit

With a loud cry, Jesus said, "Father into your hands, I commit my spirit" (Luke 23:46), and breathed his last (Mark 15:37). That final breath of Jesus released the Holy Spirit onto the earth and changed the life of the believer forever. The last breath of Jesus was the renewing of our breath of life in a spiritual sense. Jesus connects the breath, the Spirit, and forgiveness in John 20:22-23: "And with that, he breathed on them and said, 'Receive the Holy Spirit. If you forgive anyone's sins, their sins are forgiven; if you do not forgive them, they are not forgiven.'" Jesus is talking about you and me. When he breathed the Holy Spirit upon us, it came with a strict command. He wants us to forgive each other. Forgiveness takes love, and love is an essential component of both mainstream and Christian mindfulness. First, we learn breath awareness, and then we learn the rest. Please take small steps. You will learn the advanced meditations of love, kindness, and forgiveness in Weeks 3 and 4. There is no need to hurry. Right now, just focus on the breath.

The proclamation in Acts 17:24-26 connects us once again to the breath and life. God is "not served by human hands...he gives life and breath and everything else." The Lord is reminding us to anchor ourselves on his gift of life to us. The breath is a fantastic anchor for daily attention to this precious moment. Each moment is unique, so we should live each moment in thanksgiving to God. We know this is true because "all scripture is God-breathed and is useful for teaching, rebuking, correcting, and training in righteousness" (2 Tim. 3:16). The Bible and the breath are connected.

Breath Awareness and Science

Research shows that breath awareness changes the brain and reduces stress and anxiety by activating the sympathetic and parasympathetic nervous systems.[20] That is why the breath is fundamental for addressing stress and anxiety: because it directly affects the nervous system. Telles and colleagues noted that breath awareness reduces the heart rate, relaxes the digestive system, and slows the fight or flight response.[20-22] That is how God designed you. Staying in fight or flight mode all day everyday causes anxiety, and God did not create us to remain in a state of stress and worry. If you stay in fight or flight mode, you create a hold on your growth, and the Lord did not create us for that either.

When tension overtakes you, and you forget you are tense, the result is unconscious tension. Take a moment to unclench your jaw, release tension around your scalp, your shoulders, your thighs, and your feet. There is no need to carry this tension. Ease out of it, paying attention to the release in the muscles, and how this feels in the body. Find the breath in your nostrils. That is all it takes to get ready to focus on the breath and break up the stream of taken-for-granted thoughts. Later, when you take the time to just focus on the breath, it will be a familiar friend.

Striving to solve problems and avoid danger is a stressful endeavor. Humans automatically respond to threats in their environment and act on them either consciously or subconsciously. It keeps you alive, but it is not necessary to live moment-by-moment in a state of tension. Breath awareness slows things down, interrupts the constant stream of thoughts. Breath awareness can also improve decision-making ability.[22] If you are trying to make a decision, it is better to slow down and focus on the breath for about ten minutes a day to reset the brain, let go of the automatic tension, and focus on making the right decision. There are so many more examples from science that support your friend, "the breath." Still, each piece of evidence strengthens the assertion that breath awareness is the foundation of meditative practice. After you build your breath awareness, imagine the impact of coupling breath awareness with all the other methods we will discuss in the following chapters

For just a moment, once again, pay attention to the air moving in and out of your lungs as you breathe. Focus on the breath either through your nose or your chest rising and falling. Begin to unwind the holds of anxiety on your mind and body. Just practice becoming aware of your breath when you can. In a practical sense, you must breathe to live. In a philosophical sense, you breathe to remember your connection to humanity, or you become mindless. The breath is neurological, physiological, and spiritual. You are physiologically dependent on breathing to survive, and you are spiritually reliant on the breath to be mindful of your humanity, your forgiveness, and your existence. Now that you know about your breath in a new and intimate way, you should be able to focus on it with a renewed sense of awareness. I can tell you from experience, with practice, you can learn to focus on the breath. Remember, our goal is to focus on the breath, not to block thoughts. When you have thoughts, it does not mean you are failing at meditation. It means you are living, and that is a good thing. Now, let's get started by practicing this first important step.

Meditation Practice
Basic Breath Meditation

For the audio guide to this meditation, go here: https://timatkinson.net/christian-meditations/.

As noted, one of the foundations of meditation and mindfulness begins by training your mind to focus on an object of meditation. The breath is the most natural object on which to focus because it is always with you and because it reminds you of the miracle of daily existence. We can focus on the fact that God gives us each and every breath. It's okay to read this meditation to get a feel for the techniques, but you will eventually want to listen to the audio for guidance.

Sit: To begin a breath meditation, I recommend sitting in a chair with excellent support. Sit in an upright and alert position. Sit in a dignified way as you might if carrying on a conversation in your living room. Just place your hands in your lap or on the armrest of the chair. Choose whatever is comfortable for you.

Eyes: Now close your eyes; you are finding the breath at the nostrils. If closing your eyes is not suitable for you, then keep your eyes focused on your lap in a soft gaze.

Scan: Now scan your body for any tension. You are releasing the tension in your scalp, your jaw, your shoulders; softening your stomach, thighs, and calves; feeling your feet making contact with the floor, and softening them; feeling gravity's pull, holding your body to the chair.

Find Breath: Now find your breath, realizing you don't have to force it, just tracking the breath in and tracking the breath out. Just letting your body's automatic controls take over the breath. Your body will inhale when you need to inhale, and your body will exhale when you need to exhale without any effort on your part. Begin to notice when your body makes the transition from exhale to inhale—living in the moment between breaths, noting with curiosity what your body is doing during these moments.

With each cycle of breath, say in your mind, "God gives me life."

Inhaling, following the natural breath.

Exhaling, following the natural breath.

Curiosity: Become curious about the breath, noticing the coolness and freshness as you breathe in through your nostrils, and noticing the warmth of the breath as you breathe out. Remember the nostrils are a focal point for the breath. Remember that God made the breath.

With each cycle of breath, say in your mind, "God gives me life."

Inhaling, following the natural breath.

Exhaling, following the natural breath.

Thoughts: If your mind begins to wander, it is entirely okay. There is nothing wrong with thoughts. That is what your brain does! It means you are alive. Remember, as you practice, the thoughts will become less prominent.

Gently, now, you are returning to the breath.

With each cycle of breath, say in your mind, "God gives me life."

Inhaling, following the natural breath.

Exhaling, following the natural breath.

Exercise: The exercise of moving from your thoughts to the breath *is* the exercise of meditation. You are training your brain to stay focused on a single object instead of allowing your mind to run ideas and thoughts together in a constant stream.

Remembering the Biblical teachings of the breath, we breathe. Repeat.

Deep Breath Practices

For the audio of this meditation, go here: https://timatkinson .net/christian-meditations/

The following deep breath practice helps you calm down in the moment:

Inhale short: Take one deep breath in, counting 1, 2, 3, and hold until your body wants to exhale.

Exhale extended: Exhale slowly, counting 1, 2, 3, holding until your body naturally wants to breathe in.

Inhaling short: Inhale, counting 1, 2, 3, and hold until your body wants to exhale, making a note of the sensations as the body transitions from inhale to exhale.

Exhale extended: Slowly exhale, counting 1, 2, 3, 4, 5.

Repeat as many times as you like.

Time: You can do this for one to ten minutes.

Feeling: Note the sensations your body feels on the inhale and exhale.

You can also incorporate these deep breaths in the longer meditations, as you will see in the later chapters.

Encouragements and Reminders

Use the basic breath meditation as much as you want in order to increase your focus. Start with ten minutes a day for as long as you can. When you are ready, make a transition to twenty minutes. And only when you are ready, make a transition to thirty, then to forty. Follow the guide below. There is no need to hurry. Research tells us the longer the better. Mindfulness Based Stress Reduction programs typically recommend forty minutes per day, or as much as you can.

Sample Basic Breath Training Schedule

Week 1

Monday-Wednesday: Set a timer. Start with ten minutes, whenever it is convenient for you. Practice focusing on the breath. Extending space between the thoughts.

Thursday and Friday: Try twenty minutes both days.

Saturday and Sunday: Go back to ten minutes and extend the space between your thoughts.

Week 2

Monday-Wednesday: You should be feeling pretty confident by now! If not, do not worry about it and go back to ten minutes. It is okay. If you can, set your timer for twenty minutes, following the directions above.

Thursday: Try for thirty minutes!

Friday-Sunday: Keep going, using twenty minutes as the goal.

Week 3

Monday-Wednesday: If you are feeling good about your progress, set the timer for thirty minutes for these days.

Wednesday: Go ahead and feel what it is like to do forty mins! If not, do not fret. Don't beat yourself up. Do not create more holds on your body and mind.

Friday-Saturday: Set the timer back to thirty minutes.

Week 4

All week, shoot for forty minutes. If you are having trouble focusing on the breath during this time, just go back a few weeks and try shorter periods of time. Do what works for you!

Sensations Workshop

Write about your experiences and insights with breath awareness.

1. How are you uwinding the holds of continuous thoughts?

2. What happens in the transition between thoughts and breath?

3. What does the transition from out-breath to in-breath feel like to you? What are the sensations?

The Body – Unwind from Physical Tension

You can advance your mastery of meditation when you realize that everything around you, right now, represents this present-moment experience. "Now" does not include the past or the future. I believe the next thing you should learn in meditative practice is body awareness, learning to experience the complex network of senses and organs and systems that God gave you so you can experience "now" the best way possible. You can become a master at focusing when you understand that all the sensations, sounds, temperatures, and experiences you encounter during meditative practice are themselves objects of focus. The present-moment experience also includes the way you feel when you experience sadness, anger, anxiety, depression, pain, or other emotions and sensations. That is why I believe this stage is a bit more advanced than just breath awareness, so do not be discouraged if these concepts do not come to you quickly. You can always return to the breath at any time without shame or guilt. Entire meditation practices are built on the breath anyway, so it is okay to take your time. I recommend it! Focus on the body right now by just experiencing the way gravity pulls you into your chair, the temperature of the room, and even the sounds around you. All are part of this present-moment experience. As you do this, extend the space between each thought; just be still and know that God is there with you. You do not have to do anything right now but *be*.

Body awareness is essential for mindfulness practice because it augments most other meditation practices by training your brain to focus on the "conscious awareness" of the whole body. Many people use their mind, beliefs, memories, and attitudes in the act of body awareness.[23] The breath is an anchor, but so is the rest of the body and its functions. When you learn to use the body as an anchor of awareness, you can start easing more holds of stress and anxiety. In this chapter, you will learn what the Bible says about the body, gain body awareness, discover how the body and spirit are connected, and learn how to sit still in your body and sense life working around you, as gravity keeps you down to earth. If you are uncomfortable talking about the human body or have past trauma about the body, you can skip this chapter. If so, I send my loving kindness to you and pray for healing for you.

God breathed life into creation by his nostrils, the focal point of the breath. The nostrils are part of the body, and the rest of the body also plays an essential role in how we develop mindfulness. We want to develop mindfulness of the body in this present moment, experience the world more deeply, increase our spatial awareness to include the experience of temperature, light, sound, and smells. This includes the sensations of breath and what is going on inside the body, too. You will learn to take time to simply experience inhabiting your God-given body and the rest of creation around you. You are in fact taking a moment to interrupt problem solving and thinking in order to stop and simply observe God's creation and your connection to creation. All that is required is your senses. Experience the world around you now, whether hot, cold, or filled with the sounds of nature.

Body awareness plays both physical and symbolic roles in your life from a biblical sense. Most fundamentally, the Bible presents ideas of nakedness and the realization of nakedness and the body as a sense of body awareness at a very visceral level. We are embarrassed or feel exposed if we think people can see our bodies. When clothed, we do not think much about the body at all. When unclothed, it is sometimes hard not to think about the body. But most of all, because you are a Christian, you do not have to feel embarrassed or exposed. Learning to see your body as a temple of the Holy Spirit might be augmented by becoming more aware of this thing we call the body.

Body Awareness
After Adam and Eve ate from the forbidden tree against God's warning, "the eyes of both of them were opened, and they realized they were naked; so they sewed fig leaves together and made coverings for themselves" (Gen. 3:7). There was a time when they were *not* aware of their bodies, and then in Genesis 3:7, they were suddenly very aware of the body to the extent they felt they needed to cover it up. That is radical, immediate body awareness; they had to take an instant account of themselves. The Bible uses this metaphor several times to explain what it must feel like to fall away from God's favor. We feel guilt and shame, and we want to hide. But as Christians, we know that we are free from this guilt because of Jesus. We do not have to hold onto guilt or be embarrassed, and mindfulness helps us move past these stressors.

Because of body awareness, readers of the Bible are surprised to read that "Adam and his wife were both *naked*, and they felt *no* shame" (Gen. 2:25). How could that be? We have no context of not being ashamed like this. The fact of the matter is, we put on clothes every day and never really think about the body. Just like the breath, we take the body for granted most of the time, yet the body continues to function with no effort on our part. Most of the time, the body goes unrecognized because our minds are captured by a multitude of daily interests, problems, regrets, and worries. The mind that is constantly cluttered does not take time to slow down and ignores the body to a fault. When we ignore

our bodies, we dehumanize ourselves a bit. We are more like ro-
bots than living beings. We can use body awareness to interrupt
the daily flow of thoughts.

In some contexts, we are aware of other people's bodies, too,
especially in terms of their proximity to us. Remember when
Noah became intoxicated and fell asleep naked in his tent? Ham
found him in the tent, and he told Shem and Japheth about it.
They were so embarrassed that they walked into Noah's tent
backward so they would not see Noah naked and covered him
up (Gen. 9:23). Our behavior around nakedness is a component
of body awareness. In this case, though, it may be a matter of
interpretation. We are first ashamed, then, realizing God already
forgave us, we no longer have to carry the shame. But the shame
tends to capture our minds away from becoming aware of what
our bodies are doing in the present moment.

I understand that nakedness can render negative connotations, too, and that makes us not think about it. But my question
is, why should we be negatively aware of the body? Because of
these issues, we think little about the body unless we are working out, dieting, in pain, sick, or feeling pleasure. Now, I am
not suggesting we walk around naked to get to body awareness
and instant mindfulness; I am merely suggesting that when you
meditate, you should become aware of your wonderfully made,
God-given body to assist in focusing on the multiple sensations
you can experience as you sit still and meditate on the gifts from
God. Body awareness is another way to slow down and interrupt
our automatic existence, and to become better at not running on
automatic.

The skin is the largest organ in the body. Its senses are always active. It protects, feels, and senses inside and out. It de-
tects hot and cold temperatures, and can sense the environment
using a multitude of nerve networks. The skin senses the fibers
of clothing against your body. Take a moment and become aware
of the way your clothes feel on your skin right now. What about

temperature? Cool? Warm? Does your skin tingle when you think about your shoulder, arm, or leg? Does it feel warm when you cast your focus on the different parts of the body? Just become aware of these sensations as you practice body awareness.

Body and the Spirit

Nakedness can imply a lack of mindfulness or mindlessness toward the Christian attitudes of daily living taught by Jesus. Throughout the Old Testament and some of the New, nakedness demonstrates vulnerability, shame, and condemnation. As stated in Romans, we learn that the love of Christ saves us from "nakedness," and the term seems to take on two connotations: physical nakedness and spiritual nakedness (Rom. 8:35).

Further, 2 Corinthians 4 brings this out in a clear way: "Because we do not wish to be unclothed but to be clothed instead with our *heavenly* dwelling." Revelation 16:15 also addresses spiritual nakedness when it says, "Look, I come like a thief. Blessed is the one who stays awake and remains clothed, so as not to go *naked* and be shamefully exposed," which is an echo of the spiritual and physical nakedness Adam and Eve felt after they had eaten the forbidden fruit. When God comes to visit, if nothing else, you should be spiritually clothed, gracefully practicing the attitudes that Jesus gave us. Mindfulness supplements prayers and strengthens your practice of the attitudes of Jesus.

So, what is spiritual nakedness, and what does it have to do with mindfulness and meditation? Well, spiritual nakedness is likely marked by "hatred, discord, jealousy, fits of rage, selfish ambition, dissensions, factions, and envy" (Gal. 5:20-21). All of these attitudes are the antithesis of mindful daily living. All of my mindfulness colleagues, both religious and secular, know we must be the antithesis of these fundamental problems with the world to practice mindfulness. It is time to become mindful of our automatic reactions to the things going on in the world. Being mindful of your hate welling up inside you when people disagree with your point of view, or being mindful of the way envy feels when you see people who have more than you. Your rage on the highway comes in check under mindfulness. One informal mindfulness strategy you can follow in traffic, during rush hour, is gauging the tension of your hand on the steering wheel and noticing how your jaw clenches when you drive. Softening them in the name of God, letting go, and unclenching your jaw eases tension.

Body and the Fruit

What does it mean to clothe our body with our heavenly dwelling? What does it mean to be spiritually clothed? We find the answer in Galatians 5:22-23: "The fruit of the Spirit is love, joy, peace, forbearance, kindness, goodness, faithfulness, gentleness, and self-control. Against such, there is no law." The solid core of mindfulness and Christian action is to mindfully clothe yourself with love, joy, peace, kindness, and goodness. We dig into that in the following chapters.

Awareness of the body is examining, sensing, and feeling your internal and external environments both physically and spiritually, and being thankful to the Lord that he gave you these senses to explore his creation viscerally. Practice tuning in to your body's senses. Remember the gravity holding you down in your chair; the weight of your body in the chair. Feel the sensations. Examine your spirit. What do you spend time thinking about? Are you thinking how God wants you to think? If not, do not judge yourself. Simply empty your mind of these negative feelings and refill it with gentleness, love, and kindness. Some people feel an immediate release of tension in the body when they replace negative thoughts with those of love and kindness for themselves and others. You do not have to live a life of constant negative thinking.

It is not surprising that Christ is interested in self-care, because when we are spiritually exposed, we are hurting others.

We are hurting ourselves; we are not experiencing creation as he intended. This discord causes anxiety. When life is confusing, clothe yourself with the heavenly dwelling. Paul emphasized this, saying, "Or do you not know that your body is a temple of the Holy Spirit within you, whom you have from God? You are not your own..." (1 Cor. 6:19). We take the body for granted most of the time but when we meditate and focus on the body, a new awareness of importance emerges. Paul gives us further instructions for how to protect ourselves by taking on the full armor of God: the belt of truth (become aware of your waist), the breastplate of righteousness (become aware of your torso), shoes of peace (become aware of your feet), the shield of faith (become aware of your arms), the helmet of salvation (become aware of your scalp and head), and the sword of the Spirit (become aware of your hands) (Eph. 6:10-17). Do we not see that when walking in faith, we walk with the whole body, not just the mind and the heart?

Body Awareness and Science

Understanding what the Bible says about the body and how to clothe our bodies in righteousness helps us find the mindset for body awareness from a Christian perspective. When you think about the body and its wonderful sensations, there should be no doubt for the Christian that God created these sensations in us for a reason. Further assisting us in this journey toward greater body awareness and enhanced mindfulness practice, we find that science backs up what the Bible says. Studies provide some evidence that body awareness helps us open up to more positive and healthy ways of dealing with negativity instead of dwelling on and blowing up the negativity in our lives.[23]

No one promised us a trouble-free life, and we often find ourselves frustrated because life is indeed not perfect. We cannot control everything, which increases our negative thinking. But we can in fact deal positively with aches and pains, anxiety, stress, and burnout. Often our adverse reaction to our troubles only makes them worse, whereas body awareness and mindfulness give us tools to shift our thinking. Trying to push away pain might be worse than drawing toward it, or learning about what pain is telling us, or where pain manifests itself in the body. The same studies show some evidence that body awareness, such as focusing on how the emotions "feel," actually helps us learn to self-regulate our emotions and worries.[23] For instance, it might seem counterintuitive, but when I learned to focus on how and where the anxiety "felt" in my body, I learned that the physical sensations were temporary, just a series of misfiring electrical impulses in my brain causing a false feeling of tension in my chest. Often the anxiety is the result of thoughts that are only "what ifs" and regrets, and not grounded in any form of current reality. The feelings that accompany these false positives are only temporary. We can heal them.

For the program I am presenting here, we can practice body awareness by focusing on the way our body feels as it functions. When it comes to sadness, fear, etc., we do not want to think about how bad we feel, and then feel sorry for ourselves. That makes things worse. But we do want to truly understand how the emotions feel in the body. Where exactly is this anxiety you are feeling? The jaw? The chest? The stomach? It is very similar, in fact, to how you can sometimes feel your heartbeat in your chest, or your tongue in your mouth, or food going down your throat, and yes, bowels. We feel our body working all the time. The absolute best stance to have about all these sensations is to adopt the curious mind. Ask yourself what is happening inside or outside? How and why did God create this system? Simply try to understand and explain these sensations when they arise. A more crude example is burping: when you are about to belch, you can feel the air rising in your esophagus and you can sense when the air will be released. That is a form of body awareness. I knew many college friends who had excellent body awareness when it came to burping; they could slow the release of the air to extend the crudeness of it. They must have had wonderful awareness. Some might have laughed. Even laughing is associated with several sensations in the body. How does it feel to sing? And finally, pain is a sensation we can feel inside and outside the body.

Mindfulness teaches us to focus on an object of meditation for an extended period. For most of this program, we will do a mini body scan to settle into the body when we do each meditation, and we will focus on critical areas of sensation: skin, head, heart, lungs (the breath), stomach, joints, and muscles. If you want to tune into other organ systems, that is fine. Whatever God-given system you want to focus on is fine as long as it helps you with body awareness.

Meditation Practice

The Body Scan Meditation

You can find the audio for this meditation here: https://timatkinson.net/christian-meditations/.

As noted, the foundation of meditation and mindfulness begins by training your mind to focus on an object of meditation. The breath is the most natural object to focus on because it is always with us and it reminds us of the miracle of daily existence. Still, the body is also a tool for meditation by bringing other sensations into your present awareness as you meditate, including sensations your thoughts and feelings bring to bear. It's okay to read this meditation to get a feel for the techniques, but you will eventually want to listen to the audio for guidance, so you can focus on the meditation yourself.

Everybody is different! If you cannot start with your feet, start with your scalp, or start with your hands. It does not matter. Just keep track of the parts you are scanning and move to each one!

Sit: To begin a breath and body meditation, I recommend sitting in a chair with good support. Sit in an upright and alert position. Remember to be alert and relaxed. Sit in a dignified way as you might if carrying on a conversation in your living room. Sometimes I say, remember to be alert as the Holy Spirit is also with you. Just place your hands in your lap or on the armrest of the chair. Choose whatever is comfortable for you and pay attention to the breath and the body.

Eyes: Now, closing your eyes, begin to find the breath at the nostrils. If closing your eyes is not suitable for you, then keep your eyes focused on your lap in a soft gaze.

Scanning the body for tension: Scan your body for tension, releasing the tension in your scalp, your jaw, your neck, your shoulders, your stomach, your legs, and your feet. Release any tension in those areas and soften them. Take a moment to focus on the muscles in your arms. Release any tension and soften. Focus on the muscles and joints in the legs.

Feel gravity's pull: Feel God's gift of gravity pulling you into your chair by feeling the weight of your body as it contacts the chair; feeling the sensations of your feet on the floor.

Temperature: Make a note of the temperature of your surroundings.

Left foot: Scan your left foot from the tips of your toes to the heel. Examine the beautiful creation of the left foot. Notice its bones, blood vessels, and tendons, and give thanks silently to the Lord for his creation.

Right foot: Scan it from the tips of your toes to the heel. Examine the beautiful creation of the right foot. Notice its bones, blood vessels, and tendons, and give thanks to the Lord for his creation.

Thoughts: If your mind begins to wander, *it is entirely okay.* There is nothing wrong with thoughts. That is what your brain does! It means you are alive. You are functioning as God intended.

Just recognizing this fact is the exercise of meditation. Just gently return to the body scan.

Holding both feet in your awareness, soften them, being thankful to God.

Left calf: Scan it from the heel to your knee. Examine the beautiful creation of the left calf. Notice its bones, blood vessels, muscles, and tendons, and give thanks to the Lord for his creation.

Right calf: Scan it from the heel to your knee. Examine the beautiful creation of the right calf. Notice its bones, blood vessels, muscles, and tendons, and give thanks to the Lord for his creation.

Right thigh: Notice its bones, blood vessels, muscles, and tendons, and give thanks to the Lord for his creation.

Left thigh: Notice its bones, blood vessels, muscles, and tendons, and give thanks to the Lord for his creation.

Waist and pelvis: Notice their bones, blood vessels, muscles, and tendons, and give thanks to the Lord for his creation.

Torso, chest: Note the organs that God fearfully and wonderfully made. You can go more in-depth here for all the organs you can remember, scanning each one.

Shoulders: Soften. Note the sensations. Notice the bones, blood vessels, muscles, and tendons, and give thanks to the Lord for his creation.

Neck: Soften. Notice its bones, blood vessels, muscles, and tendons, and give thanks to the Lord for his creation.

Left arm: Notice its bones, blood vessels, muscles, and tendons, and give thanks to the Lord for his creation.

Right arm: Notice its bones, blood vessels, muscles, and tendons, and give thanks to the Lord for his creation.

Face: Notice its bones, blood vessels, muscles, and tendons, and give thanks to the Lord for his creation.

Scalp: Notice its bones, blood vessels, muscles, and tendons, and give thanks to the Lord for his creation.

Exercise: The exercise of moving from your thoughts to your body *is* the exercise of meditation. You are training your brain to stay focused instead of allowing it to run ideas together in a constant stream.

Remember the biblical precepts and the attitudes of Christ. Thank you, God, for this wonderfully made body.

Finish.

The Armor of God Meditation

You can find the audio here: https://timatkinson.net/christian-meditations/.

The body acts as a good tool for meditation by allowing you to bring in other sensations as you meditate, not just the breath, but sensations your thoughts and feelings bring to the table. It is okay to read this meditation to get a feel for the techniques, but you will eventually want to listen to the audio for guidance and cadence.

Stand: If you can stand, stand with your arms relaxed at your side. If you must sit, sit in an upright and alert position as discussed before.

Eye Focus: If closing your eyes is not suitable for you, then keeping your eyes focused on your lap in a soft gaze is fine.

Scan the body for tension: Scanning your body for any tension, you are releasing the tension in your scalp, your jaw, your neck, your shoulders, your stomach, your legs, and your feet. Release any tension in those areas and soften them. Think of each joint in the legs and arms; release the tension if you have any. There is no need to carry the tension.

Feel gravity's pull: Feel God's gift of gravity, pulling you to the ground.

Temperature: Make a note of the temperature of your surroundings. Cool. Warm. Hot. Cold.

Standing firm: With gravity holding you down, you are standing against the forces of evil, which are "hatred, discord, jealousy,

fits of rage, selfish ambition, dissensions, factions, and envy"
(Gal. 5:20-21).

Waist and belly: Putting on the belt of truth, scan your waist
and belly: the skin, the organs, noticing the sensations and feeling the sense of protection and truth.

Thoughts: If your mind begins to wander, *it is entirely okay.*
Remember thoughts are healthy. Give praise to God that you are
alive. You are gently returning to the body scan.

Chest: Putting on the breastplate of righteousness, scan your
chest, your organs, your muscles, your skin, sensing the protection of righteousness against evil.

Left foot: Put on the gospel of peace and scan the foot, the
bones, vessels, tendons, and note the sensations.

Right Foot: Put on the gospel of peace and scan the foot, the
bones, vessels, tendons. Sensations.

Arms: Holding the shield of faith, scan the arms. Muscles, tendons, vessels. Note the sensations. Feel your faith grow as you
stand still in God's presence.

Head: Put on the helmet of salvation. Scan the head, the scalp,
the face, the jaw (relaxing them), studying the neck, and releasing tension knowing that your salvation rests with Christ at the
center of your temple.

Mind: Grasp, now, the sword of the Spirit and mindfully clothe
yourself with love, joy, peace, kindness, and goodness—the fruits
of the Spirit. You are releasing negative thoughts.

Exercise: The exercise of moving from your thoughts to your
body *is* the exercise of meditation. You are training your brain to
stay focused instead of allowing it to run ideas together in a constant stream. But you are also training your mind to recognize
stillness and the presence of peace.

**Remember the biblical precepts and the attitudes of Christ.
Thank you, God, for this wonderfully made body and for pro-
tecting me with the armor of God.**

Finish.

Eating Meditation

You can find the audio here: https://timatkinson.net/christian
-meditations/.

Choose: Find a raisin, grape, or a piece of dark chocolate
(avoid milk chocolate). Most people choose raisins. In some of
my classes, I use dark chocolate.

Sit: Sit in your meditation position with your object in front of
you on the table or desk.

Observe: Without touching it, just notice the color, smooth-
ness, ridges, angles, marks, perfections, and imperfections. Take
into account the overall shape of your object. Think of the detail
that God put into making it, and the processes he created for
generating more and more. It could be man-made or grown on a
vine or in the ground. All of them are God's design.

Hold: Now, pick up the object and hold it in the palm of your
hand. Feel the weight and the sensations of the object touching
your hand. Hold the object between your fingers, turning it in all
directions, observing all sides.

You are closing your eyes, now.

Smelling: Slowly bringing the object to your nose, inhale as
if sniffing a fine wine. You are observing the scent and observing the smells and lingering on these sensations. How did those
sensations get there? What was the process? How wonderful is it
that these aromas arise in your nose, tantalizing your taste buds?

Taste: Now, gently placing the object on your tongue, letting
go of any expectations, let the flavors arise. Letting the flavors
surprise you. *Do not chew yet.* Just hold it there in your mouth,
noting the sensations of the object on your tongue. Smooth?
Ridged? Hard? Hot? Cold? If any flavors arise, we are just making
a note of them, and focusing. You are labeling them if you can.

If you have a piece of chocolate, just allow the chocolate to
melt a little, letting the smooth chocolate melt over your tongue.

Think now of all the processes involved in bringing this food
to you. You are thanking the Lord. Thanking the workers. The

engineers. The delivery system. You are thanking God for his creation and his processes.

Chewing Slowly: Chew slowly enough to observe the texture of the object as it breaks down between your teeth and scatters over your tongue. Observe the sensations in your mouth and throat as the pieces release their flavor. Observe the operation of your jaw and teeth.

Swallow: After you have thoroughly chewed the object, swallow it, but be mindful of the flavors, textures, and sensations as the food slides down the back of your throat. You are sensing the food traveling down your esophagus. You are detecting the food in your stomach and experiencing the inside functions of your body. Thank God, now, for what a wonderful experience this is, and what a wonderful creation you are.

Observe: Take a moment to allow the flavors to dissipate. Do not open your eyes until the flavor is gone.

Encouragements and Reminders

Start with once per week.

When you are ready, make a transition to twice a week.

When you are ready, make a transition to three times a week.

Eventually, make it a part of daily practice.

Write about your experience.

Sensations Workshop

Write about your experiences and insights from scanning the body. Write about the eating meditation.

1. What was your experience?

2. How does the body scan help you unwind from physical tension?

3. What did you experience during the body scan? How did you turn from thoughts back to the body?

4. Do the body scan. If a worry arises, instead of turning away from it, breathe into it and focus on it. Where does the worry live? How does it feel?

5. Try any of the body scans lying down. What happened? See Epilogue for some more ideas!

Love and Kindness – Unwind from Hate

You can increase your skills as a master meditator when you turn your focus toward other people and away from yourself. In this chapter, you will learn to expand your awareness and begin to cultivate a focus on others through love and kindness meditations. The next two chapters introduce what I think are the hardest mindfulness practices and attitudes of all: loving neighbors and enemies as yourself and forgiving others. These two issues create some of the tightest holds on our mind and spirit. Let us focus now on how to turn them loose, starting with hate and resentment.

You have found your breath, and you have learned to be aware of your body, and you see that together these practices increase your ability to combat stress and even anxiety. With daily exercise, you are on your way to mastering mindfulness and meditation. If you have been practicing, I send you loving-kindness and goodwill. I encourage you in the Lord to keep going. It is okay if you do not yet feel different. In time you will. Just keep practicing, even as you read. A proper sequence to follow as you read is to find your breath, feel gravity's pull on your body, find the tension in your body, and release the tension one body part at a time. Keep going for ten minutes or more. You now have the necessary tools to meditate, to use forever, without interference.

"Within your temple, O God, we meditate on your unfailing love" (Ps. 48:9). We have to practice God's example of love in order to be mindful of it and act it out in the world. Love is the engine that drives our daily existence and provides the foundation for the fruits of the Spirit. If we are breathing in and out and experiencing our feet on the ground, we should also be projecting love outwardly to other people. By practicing love, we can continue our healing because in exercising love, we have to love as God commanded, which some might find difficult. Loving as God loves also results in changes in the brain, and results in a healthful loving of yourself.

Do you remember what the Bible says about love? We know "God is love," and we know God loves the world, which makes love so important. Of the fruits of the Spirit, love is mentioned more times in the Bible than any of the others. Love is also a spiritual gift. When Paul wrote to the Corinthians, he outlined the spiritual gifts of faith, hope, and love, and added: "But the greatest of these is love" (1 Cor. 13:13). As Christians, one of our jobs is to learn to love and practice love in the world. God's love is unfailing, setting the example for mindful thought and action. Love drives God's forgiveness, and it should also drive ours. Focus on somebody you love as a family member, spouse, or friend, and just take a moment to see how it feels in your body when you think about them.

Love for Others

The most important lesson about love is that God did not command us to love those whom we already love, like our family and loved ones. There is no lesson in loving whom we already love. Jesus talked about the love we *should* give. He said, "If you love those who love you, what reward will you get?" (Matt. 5:46). The order of focus appears to be to love God first, then love your neighbor as yourself and love your enemies, while the love you have for family and friends remains without effort.

Love Your Enemies

We usually try not to think about our enemies, and sometimes our neighbors are frustrating to be around. These are probably some of the tightest holds on your mind. Loving our enemies is probably the hardest lesson of all. But the lesson is clear in Matthew 5:44: "Love your enemies and pray for those who persecute you." Likewise, we should even love strangers as ourselves: "The foreigner residing among you must be treated as your native-born. Love them as yourself" (Lev. 19:34). Also, "Do not seek revenge or bear a grudge against anyone among your people, but love your neighbor as yourself" (Lev. 19:18).

If it feels uncomfortable to think about these lessons, this discomfort is fantastic news. Just like when you discover your mind wandering, you realize you are alive; when you feel uncomfortable at the prospect of loving someone you do not love, you are experiencing life and humanity. You should feel something in your body when you seek to love strangers or enemies. Focus on where that feeling is in the body—that is the hold we must focus on during meditation. That discomfort indicates the starting place for growth. The wonders of the love of God reside in the ability to show love or feel love toward enemies and strangers. That is the most rigorous mindfulness exercise for Christians, too. "Hatred stirs up conflict, but love covers all wrongs" (Prov. 10:12).

At this point, it is likely evident that mindfulness and meditation go hand in hand. We exercise our mindfulness through prayer and meditation. Using the breath and the body in meditation is the physical work of calming the mind and bringing ourselves into this present moment. Bring yourself to "now." Then, letting go as God works means it requires no effort on your part to do his will. Faith is mindfulness that God is working, and that we do not have to do anything but trust him; this includes loving your enemies, strangers, and yourself.

Through neuroscientific mechanisms we touched on briefly, mindfulness slows us down and allows us to observe and pay attention. These actions change our brains and bodies to get ready to practice mindfulness in the world, which is the fruit of our efforts to pay attention to now! After slowing down, we focus, and when we focus, we can pray, and when we pray, we can participate in God's plan for our lives. Together you and God can start unwinding the holds of anxiety and other negative thoughts and feelings on your life.

Love and Kindness: How the Duo Works

I have practiced Christianity and mindfulness for quite a long time, and I can tell you the most significant growth in the brain comes from extending love and kindness to enemies and strangers. Overcoming the barriers to this experience can be such a hard practice. However, in a recent study by Hirshberg and associates, it was found that people who practiced loving-kindness were more likely to donate their time to help the researchers with other tasks than even the group that practiced gratitude. [24] If I asked you to send love and kindness to someone who is an enemy, you would likely look at me as if I had lost my mind. But it is a command of God to love our enemies. It does not mean to do anything other than send love to them in your mind. *There is no requirement to have a relationship with your enemies. All that is required is to build the capacity to love them as a human just as God loved us.* Have you practiced sending loving-kindness to someone you loathe, or hate, or dislike? It is a common practice in mindfulness, and it is an advanced technique that takes some practice, but the long-term benefits of letting go of your hate, loathing, and disdain bring you closer to God and work toward healing.

Living a life with a loving mindset produces kindness and eases the hold of hate on your heart and mind. What kindness should we show? Probably the brand of unfailing kindness that God shows us: "But show me *unfailing* kindness like the Lord's kindness..." (1 Sam. 20:14); "...he shows *unfailing* kindness to his anointed..." (2 Sam. 22:51); and the Lord himself said, "I have loved you with an everlasting love; I have drawn you with *unfailing* kindness" (Jer. 31:3). Being humans and sinners, we know that our kindness does fail, but building up our capacity to love increases our capacity for kindness—like loving enemies and strangers. It takes practice. Like lifting weights, you get stronger by showing up and repeating the exercises. Remember also that kindness is one of the fruits of the Spirit (Gal. 5:22), and it belongs in the catalog of Christian mindfulness attitudes. Love is something we build in our hearts, and kindness is something we do to show our love outwardly. In some ways, I am suggesting that showing love and kindness in plain sight might be harder than practicing love and kindness in our hearts.

We should practice this mindset because it releases the other spiritual gifts within us. Because the Lord "has shown kindness by giving you rain from heaven and crops in their seasons; he provides you with plenty of food and fills your hearts with joy" (Acts 14:17), and he has given us jobs, and children, and homes, and friends, and family, and life. We do not need to be anxious. Again, there is no call to have a relationship with the people to whom we show love and kindness. God simply calls us to be loving and to be kind, rising above the hate, disdain, and loathing, which are more akin to evil practices than Christian practices.

Meditation Practice

Love and Kindness Meditations

You can find the audio for these meditations here: https://timatkinson.net/christian-meditations/.

Meditation is a supplement, and the way you use the supplement and therapy is between God, you, and your therapist. There is nothing wrong with building your entire meditation practice around the breath and nothing else. If you are uncomfortable practicing the last part of this meditation, you should stop and just focus on the breath.

Love and kindness meditations are focused on the self as much as on others, so we start with self and move on to thinking of others. We do this because we want to establish the mind of Christ, who loves us without fail. The greatest spiritual gift is love, after all. These meditations are designed mainly to help you with the people in your life who can be a source of worry and anxiety, especially if there is a rift or a disagreement. At the same time, we use these meditations to remind us that God made us, fearfully and wonderfully, and God made our fellow man the same way. We start with loving yourself, loving a family member or friend, and when you are ready, extending love to a stranger or someone in need.

Sit: This time, sitting in a dignified way as you might if carrying on a conversation in your living room, remember to be alert in His presence because Jesus is with you always. Take a moment to practice the presence of the Holy Spirit as God does work in you using love and kindness.

Eyes: Closing your eyes or gazing in your lap, whatever is comfortable for you, you remember God's presence.

Inhaling short: Inhale, counting 1, 2, 3, and hold until your body sends the sensations to exhale.

Exhale extended: Exhale, counting 1, 2, 3, 4, 5. You are holding the breath until your body naturally wants to inhale again, remembering this is all by God's excellent design, exchanging gases in the environment and your body.

Inhale short: Inhale again, counting 1, 2, 3, and holding until your body wants to exhale.

Exhale extended: Exhale, counting 1, 2, 3, 4, 5.

Easing and softening: Now, shifting your awareness from your breath to the rest of your body, scan and release tension at the critical locations, releasing the scalp; face; jaw; neck; shoulders; stomach; legs; feet. You are softening them all.

Extending love and kindness to yourself:

Saying in your mind, Lord,

In you I am happy.

In you, I have my health.

In you, I have peace.

In you, I am calm.

You made me out of love.

Now, think of a friend, family member, or anyone close to you. Think about what makes them close to you. Think about why you love them, and make a note of where in the body these sensations of love manifest themselves. Reach out your hand, and in your mind say to your loved one:

In the name of Jesus,

May you have love,

May you have kindness,

May you have health.

May you have peace.

May you have calm.

God fearfully and wonderfully made you.

Now think of an acquaintance or someone you do not know very well, but maybe someone you encounter regularly. Reach out your hand, and in your mind say to them:

In the name of Jesus,

May you have love,

May you have kindness,

May you have health.

May you have peace.

May you have calm.

God fearfully and wonderfully made you.

Now for the advanced part. If you can, think of someone you don't know. Maybe the homeless person you saw on the street, or a person from a different country, or the stranger down the street. You do not have to seek a relationship with this person. Just find it in yourself, at this present moment, to begin to slowly send them love and kindness, remembering God's commands to love one another. Begin to think of this person as someone with whom you share God's breath of life and a shared fate. Someone who is also in pain, someone who also needs the Lord. Reach out your hand, and in your mind gently say to them:

In the name of the Lord,

May you have love,

May you have kindness,

May you have health.

May you have peace.

May you have calm.

God fearfully and wonderfully made you.

Make a note of the sensations and feelings in your body as you release uncomfortable emotions and replace them with love.

Now, bring this meditation to an end by extending loving-kindness back to yourself. Place your hand on your chest and in your mind say:

Lord,

In you, I am happy.

In you, I have my health.

In you, I have peace.

In you, I am calm.

You fearfully and wonderfully made me.

Encouragements and Reminders

It is okay if you cannot make it through this meditation at first. Work your way up to strangers and then try when you are ready, extending loving-kindness to everyone, unwinding ill feelings, and replacing them with the sense God commanded us to have in love and forgiveness in the world. Again, I agree these are some tough practices. I encourage you to work your way up to it slowly. It might take some time.

Sensations Workshop

Write about your experiences extending love and kindness. Remember, love and kindness do not necessarily require a relationship, but they do require seeking to have the mind of Christ. When you are ready, write about your progress.

Forgiveness – Unwind from Resentment

In just the last five years, over two hundred articles on forgiveness and health have appeared in the medical literature, which supports the Christian act of forgiveness as a healthy habit. Now, you can continue to grow your focus through Christian mindfulness and meditation by adding the practice of forgiveness, a powerful demonstration of love toward those who have hurt you, and a powerful demonstration of how to treat yourself. We can begin to ease the holds of resentment, find where they are in the body, and focus the power of Christ in those areas. The expectations are that we just begin. We do not have to be experts at this task right away. Take as much time as you need. It is about easing, which means we ease into it every day until we eventually experience the maximum release from resentment.

Remember, when you breathe, you should remember that other people breathe, too, just like you do, and we are all worthy of life and forgiveness. You now have a growing awareness of your breath, an expanded awareness of the body, and you have experienced the sensations of sending love for others and yourself. I hope you are growing in love and appreciation, and that you are experiencing an expanded awareness of your place in the world.

Christian mindfulness is about dialing into shared human-ity, to become more like Jesus, the founder of the faith. Is that not the ultimate goal? In this chapter, we explore the highly ad-vanced mindfulness technique of forgiveness. The importance of forgiveness, and its status as an "advanced" practice, is punc-tuated by the life of Jesus. He is the master of forgiveness and has commanded us to forgive, too. And even though "love" is mentioned more in the Bible than forgiveness, forgiveness itself is of no less importance, as it is the ultimate act of love. Using your breath, your body, and your love for others, let us learn to experience the Christian life on a deeper, more mindful level. Love requires fewer words to have an impact on life and society. All it takes is action.

Why Forgiveness Is Advanced Practice

The psalmist said we must have forgiveness to serve God. We know this as Christians. God built in us the capacity for forgive-ness, or the ability to develop it. We must forgive to be forgiven and to live the example Jesus set for us. "But with you, there is for-giveness, so that we can, with reverence, serve you" (Ps. 130:4). Looking at this further, remember that at the last supper, Jesus foreshadowed his death and blood as symbols of the forgiveness of sins by taking the cup in the presence of the disciples, saying, "Drink from it, *all* of you." My emphasis is on all because he did not say some of you. "This is my blood of the covenant, which is poured out for many for the forgiveness of sins" (Matt. 26:27-28). The disciples are like us, listening, trying to understand the deep fathoms of God's love for us through this profound act. But if we stopped in awe at his first statement, we would miss the point. It's not just about *our* forgiveness, but the forgiveness of many. Christ continues to explain how important this is for the believer, saying, "I tell you, *I will not* drink from this fruit of the vine from now on until that day when I drink it new with you in my Father's kingdom" (Matt. 26:29).

What does this revelation feel like in your body? For me, it feels like a chill from my head to my toes, because the revelation says to me that we must drink from the cup, or rather also forgive others for their sins against us, and when we do, Christ will be drinking with us *again, right now.* Isn't this exciting? He was not bidding the disciples farewell forever and saying that he would drink with them after they lived long lives, passed away, and all arrived in the Father's kingdom together many years later. No, he expected us to drink from the *fruit the Spirit, which is love and forgiveness for the rest of our days on the earth, and that each time we drank from the fruit, he would be present with us today, to drink from the cup with us, and complete this cycle of forgiveness.* Meditate on this revelation. Meditate on the breath of life, the sensations of the Holy Spirit in the body, and the love you give to others. Amen. May this revelation begin to ease the holds of resentment wherever they might hide.

The Forgiveness Cycle

What makes this meditation more special to me is that it increases our shared, collective knowledge of salvation as Christians. Zechariah's song reveals to us that John the Baptist will "go on before the Lord to prepare the way for him to give his people the *knowledge of salvation through the forgiveness of their sins*" (Luke 1:76-77). Here, we remember that Christ's forgiveness of *our* sins starts the forgiveness cycle and that we complete the cycle as we continue to forgive others of their sins, too. I want to continue to share the cup with Jesus today by forgiving others today. This does not only mean we keep coming back for our own forgiveness, but also, we continue to act as Christ did, forgiving others always so that we can share in his presence each time. Acts 13:38 says, "Therefore, my friends, I want you to know that through Jesus, the forgiveness of sins is proclaimed in you." And we do this by forgiving others so that everyone can receive the gifts from God.

Forgiveness and Grace

If we all received the gifts from God, what a wonderful world this would be. At the last supper, Jesus was trying to explain a completely foreign concept to his followers—ironically, it is still utterly unfamiliar to many of us today—and that is grace. "In him, we have redemption through his blood, the forgiveness of sins, in accordance with the riches of God's grace that he *lavished* on us" (Eph. 1:7-8). Again, the emphasis is mine. Jesus offered such an advanced, high-level sacrifice that the responsibility of the forgiven is also to forgive. It is the cycle of grace. Find the breath, the body, and feel the sensations for forgiving someone, sharing the cup with Christ again.

No one else is better than you are, and you are not better than anyone else. We share the same breath of life with others. You are on equal footing with your fellow humans when it comes to your dependency on breath, as well as on forgiveness. We share the same shames, guilty feelings, and worries. We should all learn to let go of trespasses and forgive others in life and death. Forgiveness of your fellow man is one of the most spiritual things you can do. All these practices are concepts of mindfulness, no matter the origin. These practices are mindfulness of others and their humanity, and God commanded us to follow these practices.

Forgiveness and Science

In his book *Forgiveness and Reconciliation*, Everett Worthington presents a theory of forgiveness with the idea that a lack of forgiveness can lead to stress and mental health issues.[25] Later, in the *Journal of Consulting Clinical Psychology*, Wade, along with Worthington and others, conducted a rigorous analysis of the literature on forgiveness and mental health and found that forgiveness helps reduce depression, anxiety, and increase hope among people who forgive.[26] There was a reason why Christ taught this to us. He wants us to be well, and forgiveness helps keep that promise. Again, science uncovered what he already knew at the beginning, at the end, and at every point in between. He is God, after all; "the Alpha and Omega, the First and the Last, the Beginning and the End" (Rev. 22:13).

To support Worthington's ideas, Harper and Worthington, in the *Journal of Clinical Psychology,* tested a "forgiveness workbook" designed to provide some forgiveness guidelines to individuals who had been harmed by others and the researchers found it an effective treatment for learning forgiveness on their road to healing.[27] In addition, Lee and Enright, writing in *Psychological Health,* found 128 studies showing that forgiveness had a positive effect on physical health.[28]

Forgiveness at Your Own Pace

I believe that forgiveness is not always a simple act, and that is why people avoid it. If someone hurts you, the hurt is real and can cause enduring physical and psychological pain and anxiety. That is why I believe this mindfulness and meditation practice is the most advanced stage. I encourage you to use the other methods in the book as long as you need to and slowly work your way to this stage. You can battle anxiety without this phase if you want; there is no expectation that you have to do this now, or tomorrow, or next week. But the command from Christ remains. You must build to this stage eventually.

If you do desire to reach this stage, just remember what the Bible says about forgiveness. Practice your breath to remind you of humanity (Week 1), clothe your body in righteousness (Week 2), experience the sensations of love for others and your enemies (Week 3), and when you are ready, slowly add forgiveness. Finally, when you are willing, forgive those who have hurt you deeply. It might take months or years, but mindfulness practice is a daily routine, and you will eventually arrive where the Lord wants you.

Remember, the most influential act of love is forgiveness, and the Lord commanded us to learn to love those we do not necessarily like. How many times should you forgive your brother or sister who sins against you? Jesus said, "I tell you, not seven times, but seventy-seven times" (Matt. 18:22). I do not believe he said to get there overnight, but he offers encouragement for working toward it until you are able.

Meditation Practice

You can find the audio for these meditations here: https://timatkinson.net/christian-meditations/.

Forgiveness Meditation

The forgiveness meditation is the most advanced meditation because it is often hard for us to forgive ourselves and others. We trap ourselves in guilt and shame, and we sometimes wallow in it and allow evil thoughts and actions to take over. Remember Romans 8:1: "Therefore, now there is no condemnation for those who are in Christ." This verse means God forgave you, period, and you have to accept this mighty gift. So, to begin the forgiveness meditation, and start unwinding from resentment, we begin with the acceptance that God forgave us a long time ago. Then, as with loving-kindness, we extend forgiveness to others, and finally to those whom we find it hard to forgive, such as someone you recently had an argument or disagreement with. And do this only when you are ready.

Sit: Again, calling on the Holy Spirit for help, sit in a dignified way as you might if carrying on a conversation in your living room, remembering to be alert in the presence of the Holy Spirit. Take a moment to practice the presence of the Holy Spirit as he does his work in you concerning forgiveness.

Finding the breath: When you are ready, find the breath. Notice the sensations of the breath as you inhale and exhale.

Eyes: Closed or gazing in your lap, whatever is comfortable for you.

Inhaling full: Take one deep breath in, counting 1, 2, 3, and hold until your body naturally exhales. Notice the breath in its transition.

Exhaling extended: Exhale, slowly counting 1, 2, 3, 4, 5. Hold until your body naturally wants to inhale.

Inhaling short: Inhale, counting 1, 2, 3, and hold until your body signals to exhale.

Exhaling extended: Exhale slowly, counting 1, 2, 3, 4, 5, emptying your lungs and loving the sensation of God's creation.

Shifting Awareness: Now, change your awareness from your breath to the rest of your body, scanning and releasing the points of tension. Release the scalp; face; jaw; neck. Soften the shoulders; stomach; legs; feet. You are softening the body and feeling gravity's pull and exploring your humanity in Christ.

Forgive yourself, saying,

I often deny my forgiveness in Christ.

I am forgiven in Christ, and

I forgive myself.

Forgiven in Christ,

I share in the cup of Christ each time.

Focus on the breath, and only when you are ready, ask for forgiveness from someone whom you have hurt, saying in your mind, I have caused you pain, and I am sorry. I want to make it right.

Ask for forgiveness from others in your mind, saying,

I have hurt you.

Please forgive me.

Forgiven in Christ,

Please forgive me.

We share in the cup of Christ each time.

You are turning your thoughts, now, to someone with whom you disagree or with whom you have had a falling out recently. The relationship is on rocky ground and it feels like you cannot make it right. Only when you are ready, think of where those sensations of disagreement and disdain arise in the body. You do not have to do this if you are uncomfortable, but only when you are ready.

Think of someone who has hurt you, saying,
We disagree, and I hurt.
I often deny you my forgiveness.
Christ forgave you, so
I forgive you, too.
Forgiven in Christ,
I forgive you.
We share in the cup of Christ each time.

Do not hurry your forgiveness. Make it genuine and humble every time. God will give you the strength to forgive each day because he wants you to heal. He designed you in his image, which means we have not yet discovered our capacity to forgive until we focus on it and practice it for a while. He wants you to forgive and let go as he commands. When we are working with anxiety, it is essential to let go of the past. Releasing this pain from the past sets you on the road to healing.

Encouragements and Reminders
Start with once per week.
When you are ready, make a transition to twice a week.
When you are ready, make a transition to three times a week.
Eventually, make it a part of daily practice.
Write about your experience.

Sensations Workshop

Write about where the sensations of forgiveness manifest in the body when forgiving yourself, asking for forgiveness, and forgiving others. Place your hand on those areas and give them to Christ.

Gratitude – Unwind from Selfishness

In just the last five years, over four hundred articles on gratitude and health have appeared in the medical literature, supporting the Christian acts of thankfulness and gratitude as healthy habits. Welcome to week five and our lesson on gratitude, thanksgiving, and learning to unwind from the holds of selfishness. Last week you learned the hardest lesson of all, and that is how to forgive others of a broad spectrum of wrongs, from people who slightly annoy you to those who have hurt you. You also learned to forgive yourself. You designed your forgiveness meditation practice to send forgiveness to those people, and then to make a note of where the sensations emerged in your body. If you were able to feel the two-way benefits of forgiveness in your body, and focus on it with your breath, and find your way to forgive someone who hurt you, then you are committed to participating in taking the cup with Christ. "Is not the cup of thanksgiving for which we give thanks, a participation in the blood of Christ, and is not the bread we break a participation in the body of Christ?" (1 Cor. 10:16). Be thankful because mindfulness and meditation train you to focus on the fruits of the Spirit and the love of God manifested through Christ Jesus.

If you have been practicing each day these five weeks, just enjoy loving yourself as a creation of God and for doing something for your well-being, giving thanks to the Lord for these tools and for easing so many holds that cause anxiety. I know this journey can be hard. Remember, we are not on the road to reach perfection; we are on a path to focus on an object of meditation, to be still and open our hearts to God, even if just for ten minutes a day. The result will be growth. We learn so much through our work and practice. If you find yourself with less anxiety and stress either now or down the road, "enter his gates with thanksgiving and his courts with praise; give thanks to him and praise his name" (Ps. 100:4). If not, do not fret. It takes time, and each person's pathway to mastery is different. Do not listen to your friends if they say they can meditate for forty minutes a day, because that creates new holds of envy. Be thankful for your own progress and keep going.

As long as you are doing some meditating, you are going to receive the benefits of the practice. Keep showing up, give him thanks for the breath, the body, love, and forgiveness. Keep visiting your doctor, too. Keep praying. The Lord will heal you, but in all things, give him thanks for everything. As you will see, giving thanks also helps you on the road to healing. I send lovingkindness to you in Christ every day, that you might find healing.

Thanksgiving to Tackle Anxiety

God has a simple prescription for anxiety: "Do not be anxious for anything, but in every situation, by prayer and petition, with thanksgiving, present your requests to God" (Phil. 4:6). He is talking about every situation. One way to look at thanksgiving and gratitude during mindfulness is to see it as praising the Father. Why do we spend less time thinking about the "thanksgiving" part of that verse? It is there for a reason. It helps us with stress, worry and anxiety.

It is probably no surprise to you that showing gratitude is a spiritual act as much as it is a therapeutic act. In Psalm 69, the psalmist is "afflicted and in pain," but sends praises to God, indicating that even when our lives are not going that well, somehow giving thanks and showing gratitude helps us for the best. In my mind, showing gratitude takes the focus off of yourself, and your object of meditation and mindfulness again becomes other people. This time, however, you benefit by showing your appreciation for the love people have given you, whether you know it or not. We should be thankful for the love and forgiveness of others as we know how hard it can be to make our human minds transform into loving and forgiving beings. Your object of meditation becomes those who have loved you, as well as God. "But as for me, afflicted and in pain—may your salvation, God, protect me. I will praise God's name in song and glorify him with thanksgiving" (Ps. 69:29-30). Withholding praise to God while you are afflicted can create extra stress, so we should praise him always with faith that he will heal us.

I do not believe God needs thanksgiving for his own sake, but I do think he commands you to be thankful to him and others for your well-being. It is a practice of self*less*ness. Our taken-for-granted nature is *selfishness*. Thanksgiving and gratitude place the focus on others, breaking the cycle of "me, me, me" to help us unwind from selfishness. God knows we can be afflicted and often are, and he knows what is good for us.

Be still and listen, now, and notice your breath, then your body, as you begin to feel the sensations of sending thanksgiving to those seen and unseen who have shown love and kindness to you. It completes the cycle of love and kindness and forgiveness. Gratitude is the response to love, and we should practice it. "All this is for your benefit, so that the grace that is reaching more and more people may cause thanksgiving to overflow to the glory of God" (2 Cor. 4:15).

Thanksgiving in Science

Heckendorf and colleagues, writing in the journal *Behavior Research and Therapy*, found that expressions of gratitude reduced what is known as repetitive negative thinking (or RNT), which is a component of anxiety.[29] Likewise, Kyeong and colleagues logged their findings in *Scientific Reports* noting that gratitude meditation had a positive effect on mental well-being and the ability to regulate emotions as indicated by changes in some areas of the brain.[30] I invite you back to earlier lessons where we learned that breath and body alone could change the brain and help us battle anxiety. Now I invite you to add gratitude and thanksgiving to your meditation practice so you can continue to augment your mindful approach to healing.

Meditation Practice

You can find the audio for these meditations here: https://timatkinson.net/christian-meditations/.

Gratitude Meditation

Sit: Sitting, now, in our upright and alert position, in the presence of the Holy Spirit, recognize that there is no need to call him. He is always with us; we just need to take a moment to acknowledge it, daily. Surrendering to his presence is all we need. No thoughts. No words. You are just placing your hands in your lap or on the armrest of the chair, choosing whatever is comfortable for you to be in his presence now.

Eyes: closed or gazing in your lap. Whatever is comfortable for you. Or perhaps, looking in a chair across from you, envisioning a place for Christ to sit with you.

Inhale short: Take one deep breath in, counting 1, 2, 3, and hold until your body wants to exhale. You are sitting in his presence.

Exhale extended: Exhale, counting slowly 1, 2, 3, 4, 5, and hold until your body naturally wants to breathe in.

Inhale short: Inhale, counting 1, 2, 3, and hold until your body wants to exhale.

Exhale extended: Exhale, slowly, counting 1, 2, 3, 4, 5.

Unwinding the tension: Now, shifting your awareness from your breath to the rest of your body, scan and release tension at the critical locations. Surrender to his presence and releasing the scalp; face; jaw; neck; shoulders; stomach; legs; feet. You are softening them all and remembering that God made us of water, each part liquid.

When you are ready, recall the words of Paul. Thanksgiving is a step in reducing anxiety; give thanks in all circumstances, being anxious for nothing.

In your mind and Christ say,

Thank you for the food.

The shelter.

For forgiveness,

For the breath of life,

For the armor of God,

For loving me,

For my gifts,

And for my family and friends.

Thank you for the things I often take for granted.

Being thankful for others, shift your thoughts to others to whom you are grateful:

Thank you for:

The leaders and workers,

The farmers,

The doctors and scientists,

The delivery people.

For sanitation services,

And for store workers, for restaurant workers.

(Add anyone you can think of for whom you are thankful.)

Thank you for the people I often take for granted.

Reflect, now, on the sensations in the body where thanksgiving is taking place. Sit quietly now, focusing on the breath, sensing the presence of the Holy Spirit, sending thanksgiving to God and others. Note that this is more than just a mental prayer: Take a moment to experience the forgiveness in your body and experience the sensations of doing God's will, and begin to unwind from selfishness.

Encouragements and Reminders

Start with once per week.

When you are ready, make a transition to twice a week.

When you are ready, make a transition to three times a week.

Eventually, make it a part of daily practice.

Write about your experience.

Sensations Workshop

1. Write down the sensations you discovered as you sent thanksgiving to the world in Christ.

2. Write down what it is like to sit in the presence of the Holy Spirit.

Humility – Unwind from Pride

You can achieve mastery in mindfulness and meditation if you forgive yourself for missing a meditation session. Do not judge yourself. You are human, so be proud of your imperfections as much as your achievements because they both teach us valuable lessons. It is okay to miss a day or two, and if you do miss, do not beat yourself up. The main thing is to practice as much as you can. Eventually, you will begin to see the rewards of regular practice. In the Epilogue, I provide some tools and ideas you can use to stay on track. It took patience and planning, but eventually I made meditation a habit in my daily life. I even started putting "meditation" on the calendar, along with picking up the laundry and going to meetings. If I cannot find forty minutes to an hour for meditation, I then find ten or twenty minutes, knowing that some practice is better than no practice at all. That has made all the difference in sustaining my spiritual and mental health.

By now, I hope you have great breath and body awareness, to the point that you can quickly find yourself in a meditative state at any free moment. Right now, you can experience the sensations of the breath in your nose, and of course, gravity's pull on your body, each a gift of God. It might be automatic at this point. Also, I hope you are experiencing the way love, forgiveness, and gratitude feel in the body. It is okay if you are not there yet, but as a teacher, I like to provide you with some guideposts to remind you of what you have learned and what your goals are. Please take to heart what I said about not judging yourself because God's works are beautiful, and you are "fearfully and wonderfully made" (Ps. 139:14), so you can move forward in the confidence that you are not failing. In mindfulness, showing up is the only measure of success. Working on it a little bit every day is the key to long term healing.

Humility to the Core

In this chapter, we discuss the reward of a daily mindfulness practice in humility, which starts you on the path to unwinding the holds of pride. In my opinion, humility is a core attitude in mindfulness. When we are humble, we can be open to love, forgiveness, and gratitude as a regular practice, and when we tune into these fruits and gifts of God, he can use us in surprising ways. Remember, in Numbers, there is an aside that says, "Now Moses was a very humble man, more humble than anyone else on the face of the earth" (Num. 12:3). God used him to change the face of a nation, to garner the respect of other countries, and to deliver the precepts of the Judeo-Christian faith in the form of the Ten Commandments. When I discuss humility, I mean the kind of humility where God can use you in beautiful ways. Take a moment to be humble before the Lord and consider what that feels like in the body, then take the step to humble yourself before someone in need, or someone who is not doing as well in life as you are. Maybe humble yourself (in your mind) before a homeless person you pass on the street. What does that feel like in the body? Where in the body are the sensations? "You save the humble, but your eyes are on the haughty to bring them low" (2 Sam. 22:28).

Moses is our great teacher of humility, reminding us how humility works. Moses said, "He humbled you, causing you to hunger and then feeding you with manna, which neither you nor your ancestors had known, to teach you that man does not live by bread alone, but every word that comes from the mouth of the Lord" (Deut. 8:3). His audience had been in the wilderness for forty years, the ultimate retreat.

For anyone wanting to deepen their practice, I highly recommend a mindfulness practice called the silent retreat. All attendees are required to stay silent, not speaking for five to ten days at a time, and in some cases eating only breakfast and lunch. It is humbling, and it is good. In many ways, this simulates a wilderness experience. Your body and spirit become humbled, realizing you do not need the daily comforts you currently have to survive. We take for granted our freedoms, abundances of food, and idle chatter. It is probably right to take some time to humble yourself like this at least once per year, and for at least for five days. One of my meditation teachers has been practicing ninety-day silent retreats for most of her life.

Andrew Murray said it best when he said our love for God would be measured by how we interact with humanity on a daily basis.[31] As we have seen throughout this course, we first humble ourselves before God by focusing on our absolute dependence on him through every breath. Then, we are humbled in the body and mind by his endless grace toward us in the face of our taken-for-granted daily lives and sinful natures. Further, we start our interactions with humankind by loving people that we do not typically love or think about, taking on the mind of Christ. The process is extended by forgiving others, even those who have hurt us deeply. Christ set the example by dying on the cross as the ultimate sacrifice for what we have done. Live humbly, forgive others, and express your love to others to complete the cycle of love and forgiveness started by Jesus. We drink from the cup with him. We forgive others; others forgive us; we are all forgiven in Christ, but we still have work to do. Mindfulness is a pathway to get there. We practice our relationship with Christ and others by sitting still and feeling the sensations of the emotions brought on by this holy task, easing all the holds of anxiety.

Murray reminds us that John said, "Whoever claims to love God yet hates a brother or a sister is a liar. For whoever does not love their brother and sister, whom they have seen, cannot love God, whom they have not seen" (1 John 4:20).31

The holds of pride can manifest themselves in some very demonstrative ways. When you see a homeless person or another person in need, take a moment to feel those sensations in your body, if any, that are holding you back from caring for that person. Those are the holds of pride right there. Likely, if the holds of pride did not restrain you, you would pause to have a conversation with your fellow man who is suffering and offer some help. I am not suggesting that you put yourself in danger, but I am suggesting that we focus on what it feels like when we witness suffering in our fellow man. What must that feel like to Christ? When we hold back from helping our fellow man, the holds of pride seal tighter. It is similar to the knot you feel when Jesus says, "If someone takes your coat, do not withhold your shirt from them" (Luke 6:29). Again, I do not think he is asking us not to defend ourselves or to be unwise by putting ourselves in danger. I do believe Jesus is saying that when someone takes your coat, a human is suffering and cold and maybe your shirt could help them, too. He is asking us to unwind from pride and to let go of our reliance on possessions for the betterment of humanity.

Humility and Anxiety

Probably one of the most comforting verses regarding humility and anxiety in the Bible contains the words of Jesus, who said, "Come to me, all you who are weary and burdened, and I will give you rest. Take my yoke upon you and learn from me, for I am gentle and humble in heart, and you will find rest for your souls. For my yoke is easy, and my burden is light" (Matt. 11:28-30). Jesus is telling us that his gentle and humble ways will bring us rest and free us from burdens, and if we are following the rest of his teachings, if we also become tender and humble, we can find rest in our souls and rest for others as well. Focusing on our humility in the face of humanity can bring rest to our souls. Humility is suitable for human relationships, and when our relationships are in balance, we remove another factor from the list of factors causing our anxiety. Paul says, "Be completely humble and gentle, be patient, bearing with one another in love" (Eph. 4:2). And when we do that, we are respecting each other's existence. With that come the other fulfilling practices of love, forgiveness, and thanksgiving! Peter also says, "Finally, all of you, be like-minded, be sympathetic, love one another, be compassionate and humble" (1 Pet. 3:8). When our relationships are in turmoil, it is likely because we are not following the teachings of Paul and Peter. We have to be humble before each other in the face of our humanity and mortality, not tearing each other down, and we must be open and sympathetic toward one another to make our relationships work! I believe that as soon as you lose sight of your humility and give in to the false notion of having to be right or winning at all costs, your relationships begin to erode, and you allow anxiety to prevail. I hope, however, I have provided a pathway out of this anxiety. Send loving-kindness, send forgiveness, and now humble yourself to each other as the Bible teaches.

Our mindful attitude of humility is a reward in and of itself, but as a humble person, you are not to expect a reward for being humble. I think we awaken one day, realizing that humility brings balance to our lives, and that is the reward. That might seem hard to understand, but if we are humbling ourselves only for the prize, then we have missed the point of humbling ourselves. But if we humble ourselves to make our relationships with others better, then we are healing our anxiety. Remember, "Those who exalt themselves will be humbled, and those who humble themselves will be exalted" (Matt. 23:12).

Again, I always return to Andrew Murray when it comes to humility because, in my mind, he wrote the best treatment of it.

He believed there are two phases on the road to humility. Step one is where we are doing everything we can to avoid being humble, taking the easy route, hanging on to our taken-for-granted nature, and struggling to follow the command to be humble. Step one is a step of anxiety in many ways. We are avoiding what we should be doing and avoiding the commands of God. We can be released from the stress of step one when we transition to step two. In step two, we realize that humility brings us even closer to God.[31] Paul reminds us that the grace of God is sufficient to work through these phases: "'My grace is sufficient for you, for my power is made perfect in weakness. Therefore I will boast all the more gladly about my weaknesses, so that Christ's power may rest on me. That is why for Christ's sake, I delight in weaknesses, in insults, in hardships, in persecutions, in difficulties. For when I am weak, then I am strong" (2 Cor. 12:9-10). When we meditate on humility, we are practicing the commands of God. We are doing the exercises of considering our fellow man above ourselves. It will be difficult at first, but with practice, we can get to the place where God wants us to be and ease the holds of pride.

Meditation Practice

You can find the audio for these meditations here: https://timatkinson.net/christian-meditations/.

Humility Meditations

In many ways, humility and thanksgiving go hand in hand. Take, now, a moment to consider your current station in life, being thankful for where you are, remembering the words of Peter and Paul to be grateful in all circumstances. Consider now how your actions affect others. Take a moment to examine if your actions improve the lives of others. Take a moment to pinpoint the holds of pride.

Sit: Sit, now, in our upright and alert position, and in the presence of the Holy Spirit, and recognize once again that there is no need to call him to appear. He is here and now, in this present moment. You are no longer ignoring him. Take a moment to recognize him, daily. Surrendering to his presence is all we need. No thoughts. No words. You are just placing your hands in your lap or on the armrest of the chair, choosing whatever is comfortable for you to be in his presence, right now.

Eyes: When you are ready, closing your eyes or gazing softly at your hands in your lap, begin to soften your body, unwinding the holds of tension throughout. Again, choose whatever sequence is comfortable for you.

Inhale short: Take one deep breath in, counting 1, 2, 3, and hold until your body wants to exhale.

Exhale extended: Exhale slowly, counting 1, 2, 3, 4, 5, and hold until your body naturally wants to breathe in. You are making a note of the sensations you experience during this transition of breath. You are living in the change of the breath, easing all the holds.

Inhale short: Inhale, counting 1, 2, 3, and hold until your body wants to exhale. You are experiencing the transitions of the breath, in thanksgiving to the Lord for your pleasant breath.

Exhale extended: Exhale, counting 1, 2, 3, 4, 5, until your body says to breathe in, just as God intended.

Unwinding the tension: Now, shifting your awareness from your breath to the rest of your body, scan and locate tension in the body, both large and small. Release the scalp; face; jaw; neck; shoulders; stomach; legs; feet. You are softening them all.

When you are ready, recall the words of Paul, knowing that thanksgiving is a step toward reducing anxiety, giving thanks in all circumstances, being anxious for nothing, easing now the holds of pride.

Say in your mind:

God made me and created humanity.

I share the breath of life with others.

I am dependent on God for life.

I extend my compassion to others.

I forgive others.

I love others.

I am thankful.

Inhale short: Inhale, counting 1, 2, 3, and hold until your body wants to exhale. You are experiencing the transitions of the breath.

Exhale extended: Exhale, counting 1, 2, 3, 4, 5, until your body sends signals to inhale. Feel those signals; release.

Unwinding the tension: Now, shift your awareness from your breath to the rest of your body, scanning and releasing tension at the critical locations. Release the tension, now, in the scalp; face; jaw; neck; shoulders; stomach; legs; feet; softening them all.

Say in your mind:

God made me and created humanity.

I share the breath of life with others.

I am dependent on God for life.

I extend my compassion to others.

I forgive others.

I love others.

I am thankful.

Reflect, now, on the sensations in the body where you feel humility. Sit quietly now, focusing on the breath, sharing in humanity with others. Note that this is more than just a mental prayer, but rather taking a moment to experience the humility in your body and mind as God intended. Practice the presence of the Holy Spirit.

Encouragements and Reminders

Start with once per week.

When you are ready, make a transition to twice a week.

When you are ready, make a transition to three times a week.

Eventually, make it a part of daily practice.

Write about your experience.

Sensations Workshop

Write down the sensations you discovered as you practiced your humility in Christ and started to unwind from the holds of pride.

PART 3

Program Toolbox

Rinse and Repeat – Building Your Cycle of Healing

You can build a meditation practice in as little as six weeks by using a simple plan. I appreciate that you have read this far, and I hope you are reaping the humble rewards of a practice that has become part of your daily Christian walk. In this chapter, I want to give you some tools and tips you can use to stay on track. Of course, you can always return to any of the six weeks of lessons to refresh your thoughts and wisdom behind each meditative approach. To start, I would like to provide you with my simple six-week checklist for mindfulness and meditation practice:

Six Week Checklist
1. The breath is life from God.
2. God created the body to sense this present moment.
3. You love one another in heart and mind.
4. You forgive one another in heart and mind.
5. Be thankful.
6. Be humble.

This chapter will help you stay on track by encouraging you to keep up the practices, schedules, attitudes, and preparations that I found helpful, and hopefully, you will, too.

Sacred Space

Many of my students and learners come to me with a desire to improve their studying skills in order to pass important certifying exams. One of the first things I ask them is, where do you study? Many of my learners are busy adults, and they say, "You know, at my desk," or, "At the kitchen table, wherever I can fit it in," or, "Listening to recordings on the way to work." And I usually respond with a lesson on sacred spaces. We have to find a sacred space for studying, for meditating, or for prayer. When I explain how distractions rob the brain of valuable bandwidth and show them the evidence, they immediately have thoughtful looks and say things like, "Well, I could clean out my spare room." Some say nothing, and when they see me the next time, they tell me they have cleaned out entire rooms for their sacred spaces. Part of mindfulness and meditation is to build your focus enough over time that you have no trouble incorporating distractions into your daily routine. Still, for the most part, it is indeed better to make the sacred space quiet.

The other part of the sacred space rule is to communicate to all loved ones and significant others that when you occupy your sacred space, you are not to be disturbed. Many of my learners forget to explain how vital the sacred space is for them to their families. In many ways, we need to have a sacred space for meditation and prayer. Do you have a sacred space?

Rules of the Sacred Space

1. Free of distractions.
2. You silence your phones and reminders.
3. Music only if it is not distracting.
4. Pets only if very still companions.
5. Talk to loved ones about the sacred space.

I have had learners tell me that they put a basket outside the door of the sacred space where they drop their cell phones. I have a phone that seems forever attached to my body sometimes, but I do silence it and put it away when I meditate. The sacred space is indeed essential, especially for new meditators.

Distractions

When it comes to meditation and mindfulness, there seem to be two camps: one that cannot have any distractions during meditation, and one in which distractions do not matter because they can incorporate them into the present-moment experience. I am a little bit of both. There are all kinds of distractions, from sounds and smells to people moving around and talking. I can handle the sounds and smells and people talking, but I usually do not like people walking in on me as I meditate. When you create your sacred space, I suggest that you not spend too much time dampening sounds, but do try to keep people from interrupting you. I have found that when people are in a meditative state and you walk in on them, they usually do not move, which means they are doing a good job of meditating. At the same time, it is an excellent idea to minimize interruptions from non-meditators— or invite them to meditate with you by saying, "Welcome, and please join me." The look on their face is priceless if they are not yet ready to meditate.

Incorporating Distractions

Remember, when you become aware of your breath, your body, the sensations of this present moment, and the presence of the Holy Spirit, you have entered a meditative state that will yield results. When external distractions arise over which you have no control, treat them like thoughts. Recognize the sounds, movements, interruptions for what they are, and then gently return to the breath or another object of meditation. Also, monitor your reaction to the distractions. Most of the time, they are just noises. That is all.

If you find anger or frustration arising in your body due to a distraction, remember you are always in the presence of the Holy

Spirit. Just say in your mind, "It is just noise," and return to the sensations of the breath and the body. If you do get frustrated, it is an excellent time to draw toward that experience and examine where you feel it in the body. A distraction should not make you want to transition from your humble, kind, loving state of mind. Call it what it is, and glide back to your breath.

Practice Schedule

In Week 1, I provided a sample schedule for practicing breath awareness as the sole practice. In this chapter, you can add all the other meditations for the entire six weeks. The following schedule is a little different from the one in Week 1. Either one is fine to use depending on your needs and level of experience. Increase times only when you are ready and do not beat yourself up if you cannot do the longest times. Ten minutes per day will still have effects!

Week 1 - Breath

Sunday-Wednesday: Practice breath awareness for ten minutes a day.

Thursday-Saturday: Practice breath awareness for twenty minutes a day.

Week 2 - Body

Twice per week, try practicing body scans for twenty minutes, noting the sensations in the body and sensations of the breath.

Week 3 - Love and Kindness

At least once per week, incorporate love and kindness to yourself and others. Extend love and kindness to people you do not like or do not know very well. You do not have to do this last part if you decide this is too hard. Increase as you feel more comfortable.

Week 4 - Forgiveness

Week 5 - Thanksgiving

All week, use the thanksgiving meditations and add to the list of things for which you are thankful.

Week 6 - Humility

All week, use the humility meditations.

In the sample schedule, practice increasing your Breath awareness meditation time later in the week. It is okay if you are not ready to increase the breath meditation time when the schedule suggests you switch it. It is okay to stick to ten minutes per day. Eventually, try to work up to forty-minute sessions; this is where you will experience the most significant benefit. Also, increase your Body awareness practice as you go along. I recommend starting with twenty minutes at a time because the body awareness process tends to keep you more focused than just an everyday breath meditation. Everybody is different. Then, for Love and Kindness and Forgiveness, increase your awareness of others as you feel comfortable. Never force your love and kindness or forgiveness. You can depend on the Holy Spirit to take over during these sessions. Just practice. As you can see, Thanksgiving and Humility meditations are not usually longer than ten to twenty minutes, and you can work these in with regular prayer time.

Conclusion

This book is for Christian believers who are new to meditation, but also for experienced Christian meditators who wish to have a refresher course on the core attitudes of Christian mindfulness or to align their precepts with those of Christianity. The chapters and audio include both scripture-based methods and neutral practices so that a newcomer can choose the practices that are comfortable for them.

The program is not a quick, heal-all scheme by any means. The practices outlined are just that: practices. It requires at least ten minutes a day for at least four weeks to experience the benefits. The longer, the better! Mindfulness and meditation are suited for practice in the presence of the Holy Spirit and the Word of God. They will help you battle anxiety, stress, and worry. This book is a ready program of meditation that is grounded in Christian thought and sentiment from the Bible. I hope it will bring you closer to God, strengthen your faith, enhance your prayer life, and finally, allow the Lord to help you with anxiety, depression, fear, relationships, eating, etc.

I have outlined my philosophy and interpretation for practicing Christian mindfulness and meditation in a way that feels safe for a person of Christian faith, and highlighted the connections between Scripture and meditation and scientific evidence. This book shows you how to be a Christian and still reap the healing benefits of mindfulness and meditation without feeling as though you are straying into another religion. Thank you for taking the time to become more mindful of Christ. I send you love and kindness, and all the best as you unwind from stress, worry, and anxiety.

For more meditations, practices, and teachings, please visit timatkinson.net

References and Other Reading

1. Anxiety and Depression Association of America. "About ADAA: Facts & Statistics," accessed February 13, 2020, https://adaa.org/about-adaa/press-room/facts-statistics.

2. Reynolds, S. G. *Living with the Mind of Christ*. London: Darton, Longman & Todd LTD, 2016.

3. Oden, A. *Right Here, Right Now*. Nashville: Abingdon Press, 2017.

4. Hickok, G. *The Myth of Mirror Neurons*, 1st ed. New York: Norton, 2014.

5. Kabat-Zinn, J. "An outpatient program in behavioral medicine for chronic pain patients based on the practice of mindfulness meditation: Theoretical considerations and preliminary results," *General Hospital Psychiatry*, 1982; 4(1):33-47. https://www.sciencedirect.com/science/article/pii/0163834382900263. doi: 10.1016/0163-8343(82)90026-3.

6. Grossman, P., Niemann, L., Schmidt, S., Walach, H. "Mindfulness-based stress reduction and health benefits: A meta-analysis," *Journal of Psychosomatic Research*, 2004; 57(1):35-43. https://www.sciencedirect.com/science/article/pii/S0022399903005737. doi: 10.1016/S0022-3999(03)00573-7.

7. Hölzel, B. K., Carmody, J., Vangel, M., et al. "Mindfulness practice leads to increases in regional brain gray matter density," *Psychiatry Research: Neuroimaging*, 2010; 191(1):36-43. https://www.clinicalkey.es/playcontent/1-s2.0-S092549271000288X. doi: 10.1016/j.pscychresns.2010.08.006.

8. Keng, S., Smoski, M. J., Robins, C. J. "Effects of mindfulness on psychological health: A review of empirical studies," *Clinical Psychology Review*, 2011; 31(6):1041-1056. https://www

.sciencedirect.com/science/article/pii/S027273581100081X. doi: 10.1016/j.cpr.2011.04.006.

9. Hoge, E. A., Bui, E., Marques, L., et al. "Randomized controlled trial of mindfulness meditation for generalized anxiety disorder: Effects on anxiety and stress reactivity," *The Journal of Clinical Psychiatry*, 2013; 74(8):786-792. https://www.ncbi.nlm .nih.gov/pubmed/23541163. doi: 10.4088/JCP.12m08083.

10. Reiner, K., Tibi, L., Lipsitz, J. D. "Do Mindfulness-Based Interventions Reduce Pain Intensity? A Critical Review of the Literature," *Pain Medicine*, 2013; 14(2):230-242. https:// onlinelibrary.wiley.com/doi/abs/10.1111/pme.12006. doi: 10.1111/pme.12006.

11. Trautwein, F., Naranjo, J. R., Schmidt, S. "Decentering the Self? Reduced Bias in Self- vs. Other-Related Processing in Long-Term Practitioners of Loving-Kindness Meditation," *Frontiers in Psychology*, 2016; 7:1785. https://www.ncbi.nlm.nih .gov/pubmed/27917136. doi: 10.3389/fpsyg.2016.01785.

12. Hofmann, S. G., PhD, Gómez, A. F., BA. "Mindfulness-Based Interventions for Anxiety and Depression," *Psychiatric Clinics of North America*, 2017; 40(4):739-749. https://www .clinicalkey.es/playcontent/1-s2.0-S0193953X1730076X. doi: 10.1016/j.psc.2017.08.008.

13. Sizoo, B. B., Kuiper, E. "Cognitive behavioural therapy and mindfulness based stress reduction may be equally effective in reducing anxiety and depression in adults with autism spectrum disorders," *Research in Developmental Disabilities*, 2017; 64:47-55. https://www.sciencedirect.com/science/article/pii /S0891422217300823. doi: 10.1016/j.ridd.2017.03.004.

14. Pbert, L., Madison, J. M., Druker, S., et al. "Effect of mindfulness training on asthma quality of life and lung function: a randomised controlled trial." *Thorax*, 2012; 67(9):769-776. http://dx.doi.org/10.1136/thoraxjnl-2011-200253. doi: 10.1136/thoraxjnl-2011-200253.

15. Linda E. Carlson, Richard Doll, Joanne Stephen, et al. "Randomized Controlled Trial of Mindfulness-Based Cancer Recovery Versus Supportive Expressive Group Therapy for Distressed Survivors of Breast Cancer (MINDSET)," *Journal of Clinical Oncology*, 2013; 31(25):3119-3126. http://jco .ascopubs.org/content/31/25/3119.abstract. doi: 10.1200/ JCO.2012.47.5210.

16. Hartmann, M., Kopf, S., Kircher, C., et al. "Sustained effects of a mindfulness-based stress-reduction intervention in type 2 diabetic patients: design and first results of a randomized controlled trial (the Heidelberger Diabetes and Stress-study)," *Diabetes Care*, 2012; 35(5):945-947. https://www.ncbi.nlm.nih .gov/pubmed/22338101. doi: 10.2337/dc11-1343.

17. Zernicke, K., Campbell, T., et al. "Mindfulness-based stress reduction for the treatment of irritable bowel syndrome symptoms: a randomized wait-list controlled trial," *Int J Behav Med*, 2013; 20(3):385-396. https://www.ncbi.nlm.nih.gov /pubmed/22618308. doi: 10.1007/s12529-012-9241-6.

18. Sullivan, M. J., MD, Wood, Laura, RN, BSN, Terry, Jennifer, MS, LPC, CRC, et al. "The Support, Education, and Research in Chronic Heart Failure Study (SEARCH): A mindfulness-based psychoeducational intervention improves depression and clinical symptoms in patients with chronic heart failure," *American Heart Journal*, 2009; 157(1):84-90. https:// www.clinicalkey.es/playcontent/1-s2.0-S0002870308008235. doi: 10.1016/j.ahj.2008.08.033.

19. Rodrigues, M. F., Nardi, A. E., Levitan, M. "Mindfulness in mood and anxiety disorders: a review of the literature," *Trends in Psychiatry and Psychotherapy*, 2017; 39(3):207-215. https://www.ncbi.nlm.nih.gov/pubmed/28767927. doi: 10.1590/2237-6089-2016-0051.

20. Telles, S., Vishwakarma, B., Gupta, R. K., Balkrishna, A. "Changes in Shape and Size Discrimination and State Anxiety After Alternate-Nostril Yoga Breathing and Breath Awareness

in One Session Each," *Medical Science Monitor Basic Research,* 2019; 25:121-127. https://www.ncbi.nlm.nih.gov/pubmed /31006767. doi: 10.12659/MSMBR.914956.

21. Telles, S., Singh, N., Balkrishna, A. "Heart rate variability changes during high frequency yoga breathing and breath awareness," *BioPsychoSocial Medicine,* 2011; 5(1):4. https://www.ncbi.nlm.nih.gov/pubmed/21486495. doi: 10.1186/1751-0759-5-4.

22. Joshi, M., Telles, S. "A nonrandomized non-naive comparative study of the effects of kapalabhati and breath awareness on event-related potentials in trained yoga practitioners," *Journal of Alternative and Complementary Medicine (New York, N.Y.),* 2009; 15(3):281-285. https://www.ncbi.nlm.nih.gov /pubmed/19243275. doi: 10.1089/acm.2008.0250.

23. Mehling, W. E., Wrubel, J., Daubenmier, J. J., et al. "Body Awareness: A phenomenological inquiry into the common ground of mind-body therapies," *Philosophy, Ethics, and Humanities in Medicine: PEHM,* 2011; 6(1):6. https://www.ncbi .nlm.nih.gov/pubmed/21473781. doi: 10.1186/1747-5341-6-6.

24. Hirshberg, M. J., Goldberg, S. B., Schaefer, S. M., Flook, L., Findley, D., Davidson, R.J. "Divergent effects of brief contemplative practices in response to an acute stressor: A randomized controlled trial of brief breath awareness, loving-kindness, gratitude or an attention control practice," *PloS One,* 2018; 13(12):e0207765. https://www.ncbi.nlm.nih.gov/pubmed /30540772. doi: 10.1371/journal.pone.0207765.

25. Worthington, E.L. *Forgiveness and Reconciliation.* New York: Routledge, 2006. http://www.loc.gov/catdir/toc/ecip063 /2005033905.html.

26. Wade, N. G., Hoyt, W. T., Kidwell, J. E. M., Worthington, E. L. "Efficacy of psychotherapeutic interventions to promote forgiveness: a meta-analysis," *Journal of Consulting and Clinical Psychology,* 2014; 82(1):154-170. https://www.ncbi.nlm.nih.gov /pubmed/24364794. doi: 10.1037/a0035268.

27. Harper, Q., Worthington, E. L., Griffin, B. J., et al. "Efficacy of a workbook to promote forgiveness: A randomized controlled trial with university students," *Journal of Clinical Psychology*. 2014; 70(12):1158-1169. doi: 10.1002/jclp.22079.

28. Lee, Y., Enright, R. D. "A meta-analysis of the association between forgiveness of others and physical health," *Psychology & Health*, 2019; 34(5):626-643. http://www.tandfonline.com/doi/abs/10.1080/08870446.2018.1554185. doi: 10.1080/08870446.2018.1554185.

29. Heckendorf, H., Lehr, D., Ebert, D. D., Freund, H. "Efficacy of an internet and app-based gratitude intervention in reducing repetitive negative thinking and mechanisms of change in the intervention's effect on anxiety and depression: Results from a randomized controlled trial," *Behaviour Research and Therapy*, 2019; 119:103415. http://dx.doi.org/10.1016/j.brat.2019.103415. doi: 10.1016/j.brat.2019.103415.

30. Kyeong, S., Kim, J., Kim, D. J., Kim, H. E., Kim, J. "Effects of gratitude meditation on neural network functional connectivity and brain-heart coupling," *Scientific Reports*, 2017; 7(1):5058-15. https://www.ncbi.nlm.nih.gov/pubmed/28698643. doi: 10.1038/s41598-017-05520-9.

31. Murray, A. *Humility*, reprinted ed. Bethany House Publishers, 2001.

Printed in the United States
By Bookmasters